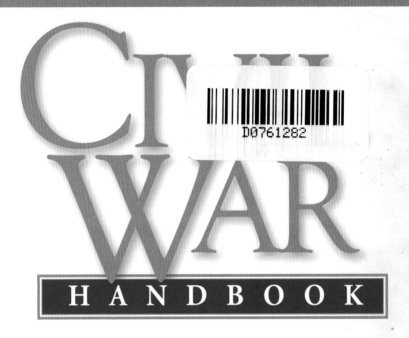

CIVIL WAR
HANDBOOK

In the lower corners of the pages in this handbook are outlined boxes. These are spaces to get your handbook canceled when you visit a park. These ink markings record the name of the park and the date of your visit. Cancellations are free of charge and are available at the Passport To Your National Parks® station usually located in a park's visitor center. For more information, please contact Eastern National at 877-628-7275 or visit www.eParks.com

Eastern National, 470 Maryland Drive, Fort Washington, PA 19034

Eastern National promotes the public's understanding and support of America's national parks and other public trust partners by providing quality educational experiences, products, and services.

Special thanks to all National Park Service personnel who helped in the production of this book.

Appomattox Court House Nat'l Hist Park
APR 09 2015
Appomattox, VA

TABLE OF CONTENTS

On April 12, 1861, the American Civil War began with the first shots fired at Fort Sumter in Charleston Harbor, South Carolina. At the time, no one could predict that the war would last four years, or that this would be "the most momentous era in American history." Neither could anyone know that by the war's end, over 620,000 Americans on both sides would never return home. Even less obvious was that by war's end, 4,000,000 enslaved people would experience a "new birth of freedom."

On May 23, just six weeks after the surrender of Fort Sumter, another, and a far more subtle war began. Three enslaved men, Shepard Mallory, Frank Baker, and James Townsend snuck away from the Confederate fortification they were forced to work on, confiscated a small boat, rowed across the harbor, and presented themselves to Gen. Benjamin Butler, the Union commander of Fort Monroe in Virginia. Since the three slaves were working on a Confederate fort that, when finished, would be aiming its guns at his fort, Butler declared the three men contraband of war—an accepted wartime measure—stating that

Bombardment of Ft. Sumter

"property" used by the enemy against the Union could be confiscated. Soon, news spread among the networks of enslaved people, and others left Confederate work sites and plantations, fleeing to Union lines. What started as an act of defiance by these three men became a revolution to end slavery, and by the end of the Civil War, some 500,000 enslaved people sought protection with the Union army and some 200,000 donned the Union uniform.

Thus, the American Civil War era was both our greatest military struggle and our greatest social revolution.

As the keepers of our national park sites, we are entrusted with preserving and maintaining over 75 parks related to this era. For almost a hundred years, we have successfully used our parks as laboratories to take our visitors back in time to provide understanding of the armies of the Union and the Confederacy as they met on the fields of battle. We have talked about who these people were who fought and died, as well as how they fought, the weapons they used, the clothing and equipment they carried, the heroism and valor of both individuals and regiments, and the suffering and devastation that the battles left behind. This mission is and always will be very important.

But even more important is providing some understanding of why they were fighting in the first place and what it meant to us as a nation. Indeed, why should we care about the Civil War? We should care, because as Mark Twain said several years after the war was over, that it "uprooted institutions that were centuries old, changed the politics of a people, transformed the social life of half the country, and wrought so profoundly upon the national character that the influence cannot be measured short of two or three generations."

It's important to look at the causes of the war, one of which was the South's incredible investment in the slave economy. In 1860, about 30 percent or 385,000 of the white population in slave states owned slaves, and of that number 12 percent owned 20 or more slaves. About 30 percent of the nation's population lived in the South, but 60 percent of the wealthiest individuals were concentrated in the South. Further, the per capita income in the South was nearly double that in the North. To place these figures in more modern terms, in the 1950s only two percent of American families owned corporation stocks equal to the value of one slave

Fredericksburg residents return to their shattered homes.
Painting by David Henderson

in 1860. To carry these statistics a little further, the value of slaves in the United States in 1860 was about $3,000,000,000, which was greater than the combined value of railroads, factories, and banks in the entire country, and greater than all land, cotton, and goods in the South. Clearly, the Confederacy was committed to protecting its economy and way of life, built upon the institution of slavery.

On the other hand, the North was just as strongly committed to preserving the Union. Like most Northerners, President Lincoln's message to Congress in December 1862 summed up their

A Union soldier reads the Emancipation Proclamation to a group of slaves.

views, that the war was being waged to "nobly save, or meanly lose, the last best hope of earth." But, in his message, Lincoln also signaled a shift in his and the Union's war aims. He was preparing to issue the final Emancipation Proclamation. In his 1862 message to Congress, the President also stated that "in giving freedom to the slave, we assure freedom to the free."

Before 1861, Americans grappled with the permanence or impermanence of the Union as a major political and constitutional question, with respected public figures taking opposing sides. The Civil War forever decided that question of union or disunion.

Although arguments about state rights did not end in 1865, discussion about the permanence of the Union halted abruptly. Although we still struggle after 150 years to define our concept of citizenship, we clearly have evolved from a nation often referred to in plural as a collection of states, to a singular and united republic.

We hope this book will whet your appetite to visit your Civil War era national parks. Each park preserves a piece of tangible history and provides compelling stories of the people—soldiers and civilians, men and women, freedmen and slaves, immigrants and Native Americans—who endured, suffered, and persevered through four long years of struggle. Their stories illuminate the military, political, social, and economic facets of the Civil War years, from causes to consequences and from battlefront to home front, for the Civil War was indeed a struggle that touched the lives of every American in the 1860s. We invite you to read, to visit, and to understand.

–Robert K. Sutton, Chief Historian, National Park Service

This romanticized depiction of Lee and Grant meeting the day after the surrender was painted by Stanley Arthurs in 1922. (Courtesy Delaware State Museums)

Tuskegee Institute was established in 1881 as a result of the outcome of the Civil War. The school was developed through the partnership of Lewis Adams, a former slave, and George Campbell, a former slave owner. They saw a need for a site to educate African Americans in rural Alabama. The school was founded on July 4 with Booker T. Washington as its first principal. Washington had a plan to train most of his students to be teachers and have them return to their rural communities to teach farming and to improve the intellectual and religious life of the people. He worked tirelessly to promote the Tuskegee Normal and Industrial Institute and established several vocational classes including brick making, gardening, and carpentry. He was a visionary and wanted to bring the brightest African Americans to the school to share their knowledge and experience. To create the agricultural department, he recruited George Washington Carver who had just graduated as the first African American at Iowa State Agricultural College. Washington and Carver, both former slaves, knew the importance of providing learning opportunities at Tuskegee. From a modest beginning in a one room shanty, the school has become a leader in providing students a comprehensive education.

Fort Bowie National Historic Site

3203 South Old Fort Bowie Road • Bowie, AZ 85605 • 520-847-2500

The ruins of the cavalry barracks

Corp. Aaron Cory Hitchcock, Company M, 1st California Volunteer Cavalry

Fort Bowie was established because of the Civil War. As the war commenced, the Butterfield Overland Trail, which had been mapped through Apache Pass because of Apache Spring, was moved to a northern route. The stage station at Apache Pass and Forts Buchanan and Breckenridge were abandoned as Confederate troops invaded New Mexico and occupied Tucson. In response to the Confederate threat, Union strategists organized volunteers to march from California. In June 1862, Lt. Col. Edward Eyre of the 1st Volunteer Cavalry, with a 140-man reconnaissance patrol, lost three men when they were attacked by heavily armed Chiricahua Apache warriors. In July, an advance command of infantry lost two more men in Apache Pass after an ambush triggered two days of heavy fighting. Reporting this fight, Capt. Thomas Roberts advised Gen. James Carleton that "a force sufficient to hold the water and pass should be stationed there, otherwise every command will have to fight for water." On July 28, 1862, the first Fort Bowie was officially established on a small hillside overlooking Apache Spring. A second, more extensive fort was built five years later just east of the first fort. Today, the ruins of both are protected by the National Park Service.

Arkansas

ARKANSAS POST NATIONAL MEMORIAL

1741 Old Post Road · Gillett, AR 72055 · 870-548-2207

Civil War firing demonstration

On the evening of January 9, 1863, approximately 30,000 Union troops led by Maj. Gen. John A. McClernand arrived a few miles below Fort Hindman at Arkansas Post. Fort Hindman was a Confederate earthwork that sat on a bluff 25 feet above the Arkansas River. Brig. Gen. Thomas J. Churchill was commander of 5,000 Confederate troops at Arkansas Post. On the morning of January 10, Union gunboats made their approach and began shelling the fort. Later that afternoon, ground troops were sent out to get in position for the assault. On January 11 at 1 p.m., the Union gunboats came up the river and began shelling Fort Hindman once more. After an hour of firing on Fort Hindman, the Confederate guns fell silent and the fort was in ruins. Union ground troops made their advance slowly and suffered high casualties. Union gunboats gained position behind the Confederate flank with a clear view of the field works. The Confederate army at Arkansas Post was surrounded, and by 4 p.m. on January 11, white flags began to wave. With a Union victory at Arkansas Post, supply boats could move unimpeded down the Mississippi River to Vicksburg.

Fort Smith National Historic Site

P.O. Box 1406 • Fort Smith, AR 72902 • 479-783-3961

Courthouse

Gallows

Established in 1961, Fort Smith National Historic Site preserves the location and stories of the early western frontier. From the founding of the first fort in 1817 to the establishment of the second fort in 1846, from the Civil War to the federal justice days of Judge Isaac C. Parker's famous courtroom and gallows, the park offers visitors a close-up view of frontier life in the 19th century. During the early years of the Civil War (1861-1863), the fort served as a staging point for the Confederacy in several battles in the West. In the later years (1864-1865), it served as a Union command center for maintaining order in the western half of Arkansas. Today, the park offers visitors a wide variety of interpretive opportunities including living history programs, ranger talks, guided walks, and educational programs.

The park's visitor center is open daily from 9:00 a.m. to 5:00 p.m. The park is closed on Christmas and New Year's.

Deputy U.S. Marshals

PEA RIDGE NATIONAL MILITARY PARK

15930 East Highway 62 • Garfield, AR 72732 • 479-451-8122

Pea Ridge National Military Park commemorates the March 7-8, 1862, Battle of Pea Ridge that helped secure the state of Missouri for the Union. The Union Army of the Southwest with 10,500 men under the command of Brig. Gen. Samuel R. Curtis defeated the larger Confederate Army of the West with 16,000 men commanded by Maj. Gen. Earl Van Dorn. The battle began March 7 with fighting on two separate battlefields. At Leetown, Confederate Gen. Ben McCulloch and his troops, including 2,000 Cherokee, were defeated by a much smaller force of Federals under the command of Colonels Osterhaus and Davis. During the fight, McCulloch and his second-in-command Gen. James McIntosh were killed. The Confederate survivors would rejoin Confederate Generals Van Dorn and Price at Elkhorn Tavern on March 8.

Three miles to the east, Van Dorn and Price were clawing and fighting their way up the steep-sided ravines near Elkhorn Tavern. Union Cols. Eugene Carr and Grenville Dodge used the terrain to their advantage and held off the larger Confederate

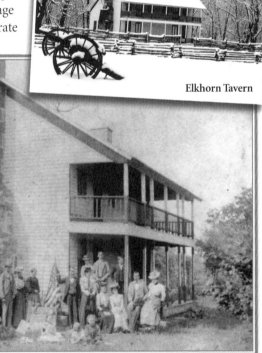

Elkhorn Tavern

Elkhorn Tavern
late 1800s

Gen. Sterling Price

Gen. Samuel Curtis

Missouri State Guard force until late afternoon when the Union left flank near Elkhorn Tavern was broken and the Federals were forced to retreat. Darkness halted the successful Confederate attack at Elkhorn Tavern. During the night, both armies prepared for the next day's battle. Van Dorn learned that his supply wagons were left far behind and his army would have little ammunition to fight with the next day.

On the morning of March 8, Union Gen. Franz Sigel opened a two-hour artillery barrage against the Confederate line. The Confederate guns responded as best they could but quickly ran out of ammunition and were forced to retire. When the barrage ended, the entire Union army charged forward and the Confederates fled from the battlefield. After the battle, Union General Curtis reported 1,384 casualties while the Confederate casualties were estimated at 2,000.

Today, the 4,300-acre battlefield stands as a monument to the men who fought and died here. The park includes a seven-mile tour road, wayside exhibits, and 10 miles of hiking trails. The park provides infantry and artillery demonstrations, and ranger talks throughout the year.

Ft. Point

Far from the critical battlefields of the East, California was nevertheless contested ground in the Civil War era. Its admission to the Union as a free state was a cornerstone of the Compromise of 1850, yet many citizens of California hailed from the South, and the retention of the wealth and manpower of the Golden State for the Union required constant vigilance. Fort Point, the only classic brick fort west of the Mississippi, was rushed to completion in 1861, its first cannon aimed towards the land to guard against possible seizure by Confederate agents. Its seaward-facing guns warded off the famous raider CSS *Shenandoah* in 1865. Alcatraz, the world's most famous prison, was built as the centerpiece of the defense for San Francisco Bay, the little island ringed with heavy artillery and crowned with a defensive citadel on its crest. The 1857 sally port and guardhouse that held the island fortress' first prison was used to jail numerous Confederate sympathizers.

24th Infantrymen, 1899

In 1866, the 9th and 10th Cavalry Regiments and the 24th and 25th Infantry Regiments came into being. The African Americans who filled the ranks of these units became known as the Buffalo Soldiers, primarily as a result of their service during the Indian Wars. That name was given to them because their Plains Indian antagonists saw that the hair on these men was very similar to the matted cushion between the horns of the buffalo. As the buffalo was sacred to these Indians, the term "buffalo soldier" was perhaps the only positive term bestowed on these soldiers. Company H of the 24th Infantry in 1899, and troops of the 9th Cavalry in 1903, were dispatched from their winter garrison in San Francisco to summer duty in Yosemite and Sequoia & General Grant national parks. These soldiers were role models because they held positions that engendered respect at a time when many African Americans still worked in jobs that were not significantly different from tasks they were given before the Civil War. African Americans were active participants in westward expansion. They were explorers, fur trappers, pioneers, homesteaders, and cowboys.

910 Wansted · P.O. Box 249 · Eads, CO 81036 · 719-729-3003

Colorado's first cavalry
regiment was formed in November 1862.
Their assignment was to guard the
Colorado Territory and its gold mines
from possible Confederate invasion
and to protect the ever-expanding
white settlements from Indian raids.
In September 1864, several chiefs of the
Cheyenne and Arapaho tribes came to
Denver in an attempt to make peace.
Territorial Governor John Evans spurned
this attempt, and referred
the matter to the military
commander, Colonel
Chivington. Thus the stage
was set for the Sand Creek
Massacre in November 1864.

Late that November,
soldiers from 10 companies,
most of whom were from the
3rd Colorado Cavalry, along
with detachments from the
1st Colorado Cavalry, traveled
in great secrecy to Fort Lyon on
the Arkansas River near present day Lamar. In an overnight march through
bitter cold, they moved in on the only group of Indians Chivington could find—
Chief Black Kettle's camp on the Big Sandy. At dawn on November 29, 1864,
they attacked, killing about 150 Indian men, women, and children while losing
10 soldiers.

Chief Left Hand, Southern Cheyenne Sand Creek family member

The massacre profoundly influenced
U.S.-Indian relations and the structure of the
Cheyenne and Arapaho tribes. Legislation to
establish a Sand Creek Massacre National
Historic Site began in 1998. The site was
established in 2007 to preserve and protect the
cultural landscape of the massacre and enhance
public understanding.

Use this page for cancellations or field notes.

c/o Rock Creek Park Nature Center • 5200 Glover Road, NW
Washington, DC 20020 • 202-690-5185

During the Civil War, the Lincoln administration feared an attack on Washington, D.C., from Confederates and Southern sympathizers prompting the Federal government to seize private lands with views of essential roads, bridges, and waterways. On these strategic points, Union forces quickly built a ring of earthen fortifications around the nation's capital and moved massive cannons into place. By the end of the Civil War, the Union army, civilians, and former slaves had constructed 68 forts, 93 gun batteries, 20 miles of rifle pits, and 32 miles of military roads around the capital, resulting in one of the most fortified cities in the world. Daily life in the forts focused on drilling, digging, and strengthening the fortifications, and on routine military duties. Eventually, the defenses would be challenged.

Encampment near Ft. Slocum

Typical camp life

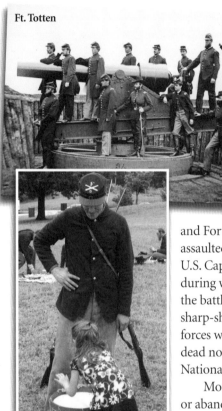

Ft. Totten

Reenactor and visitor at Ft. Stevens

On July 9, 1864, Confederate Lt. Gen. Jubal A. Early and a force of 14,000 men fought at the Monocacy River near Frederick, Maryland, and proceeded toward Washington, D.C. By July 11, they crossed the Potomac River and encountered fire from Fort Reno, Fort DeRussy, and Fort Slocum. Early's Confederate force then assaulted Fort Stevens—just six miles from the U.S. Capitol. Fighting continued for two days, during which time President Lincoln visited the battle and was nearly struck down by sharp-shooter bullets. Ultimately, the Confederate forces were rebuffed. The bodies of 40 Union dead now lie in rest at nearby Battleground National Cemetery.

Most of the fortifications were dismantled or abandoned by 1866. Although some elements surrendered to time and urbanization, many fortifications and associated lands remain protected. Within the National Park System is a ring of historic fort sites stretching from Fort Marcy in Virginia, passing through one of the largest park areas in the District of Columbia at Fort Dupont, and extending to Fort Foote in Maryland. Parks and woodlands now occupy the heights where heavy guns once scanned the horizon—and people stroll, hike, and bike where soldiers once stood guard.

Today, 19 fortification sites and a national cemetery are managed by National Capital Parks-East, George Washington Memorial Parkway and Rock Creek Park. Cancellation stamps are available at Fort Dupont and park headquarters for any of the three managing parks.

Use this page for cancellations or field notes.

Use this page for cancellations or field notes.

Ford's Theatre National Historic Site

511 10th Street, NW • Washington, DC 20004 • 202-426-6924

President and Mrs. Lincoln came to Ford's Theatre on April 14, 1865, to see the play "Our American Cousin." John Wilkes Booth also was in attendance, and was planning to assassinate Lincoln during Act 3 Scene 2. When the time came, Booth entered Lincoln's box and shot him in the back of the head. Booth jumped from the box, landed on the stage, and yelled "Sic Semper Tyrannis" (thus always to tyrants). Booth escaped across the stage and mounted a horse bound for Virginia. His flight ended 12 days later when he was fatally shot in a tobacco barn outside Port Royal, Virginia. Doctors immediately determined that Lincoln's wound was fatal, but by removing the blood clots they could keep him alive for a few more hours. Abraham Lincoln was carried out of the theatre and across the street into the Petersen House. He was laid diagonally on a bed in the back bedroom because his tall frame was too big to lie regularly. Lincoln died in the Petersen House at 7:22 a.m. on April 15, 1865. The assassination of Abraham Lincoln forever changed the history of the United States.

Ford's Theatre is still an active theatre.

Ford's Theatre

Petersen House

1411 W Street, SE • Washington, DC 20020 • 202-426-5961

Frederick Douglass was born a slave on Maryland's Eastern Shore in 1818 and was given the name Frederick Augustus Washington Bailey. He learned to read and write at an early age and later escaped to freedom in the North, changing his name to Douglass to avoid recapture. He settled in Rochester, New York, and was active in the abolitionist cause, delivering many eloquent and powerful speeches. He was a leader of Rochester's Underground Railroad movement and became editor and publisher of *The North Star*, an abolitionist newspaper. During the Civil War, he advocated for equality for African American soldiers.

In 1872, he moved to Washington, D.C., served as marshal of the District of Columbia, and was appointed recorder of deeds. In 1889, President Harrison appointed him minister-resident and consul general to the Republic of Haiti and charge d'affaires for Santo Domingo. Douglass continued to be an outspoken advocate for equal rights for everyone throughout his life.

He lived at his Cedar Hill estate from 1877 until his death in 1895. The property was added to the National Park System on September 5, 1962, and was designated a national historic site in 1988. Frederick Douglass National Historic Site helps us understand the life of the man who is recognized as "the father of the civil rights movement."

LINCOLN MEMORIAL

Washington D.C.

c/o National Mall and Memorial Parks
900 Ohio Drive, SW • Washington, DC 20024 • 202-426-6841

Built to honor the nation's 16th president, the Lincoln Memorial contains a 19-foot-high marble statue by Daniel Chester French of the Great Emancipator Abraham Lincoln. The classic white marble structure is designed in the style of a Greek temple but with its entrance on the east side instead of at either end. Carved on the walls of the memorial are the Gettysburg Address and Lincoln's Second Inaugural Address. The 36 marble columns represent the states of the Union at the time of Lincoln's death, and the names of these states are carved on the frieze above the columns. The names of the 48 states in the Union when the memorial was completed in 1922 are carved on the walls above the frieze. A plaque honoring the subsequent entry of Alaska and Hawaii is in the approach plaza.

On the day of dedication of the memorial, May 30, 1922, more than 50,000 people attended the ceremonies. Among the notables was Robert Todd Lincoln, the only surviving son of the president. Since that day, the memorial has become a national forum—the setting for celebrations, for the airing of grievances, and for commemorations.

c/o George Washington Memorial Parkway
Washington, DC • 703-289-2500

Washington
D.C.

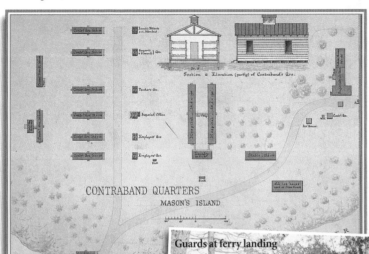

CONTRABAND QUARTERS
MASON'S ISLAND

Guards at ferry landing

Theodore Roosevelt
Island served as a refuge for
slaves who escaped or were
captured from Confederate
owners, and as a secret
training ground for the
1st Regiment United States
Colored Troops. To alleviate
overcrowding at Freedman's Village—the village
built to house and feed "contraband" African Americans in Arlington—the
Freedmen's Bureau built a spartan "employment depot" on the island—then
known as Mason's Island. Some residents found work on nearby plantations,
but many were recruited into the first regiment of
African American volunteers to be mustered into
the regular Union army in 1863. The location of
their barracks on Mason's Island was kept secret
to avoid racially motivated violence from Southern
sympathizers. These men learned military drills
at Camp Greene on the island, and later went on
to fight in numerous battles and skirmishes.

25

Florida

GULF ISLANDS NATIONAL SEASHORE

1801 Gulf Breeze Parkway • Gulf Breeze, FL 32563 • 850-934-2600
(Also located in Mississippi)

On the night of January 8, 1861, guards at Fort Barrancas in Pensacola Bay heard footsteps on the bridge to the fort and a musket was fired to sound the alarm, one of the first shots fired in the crisis. Federal troops then moved from Fort Barrancas to Fort Pickens south across the harbor and refused to surrender to state forces. A truce kept the peace as Federal reinforcements arrived offshore and hundreds of Confederate troops poured into Pensacola. Union reinforcements landed on April 13, the day after the war began.

Following a Federal raid on the Pensacola navy yard in September, over 1,000 Confederates under Gen. Braxton Bragg made a night assault on a Union camp outside Fort Pickens on October 9, 1861. Known as the Battle of Santa Rosa Island, this action led to a massive artillery bombardment by Federal army and naval forces at Pensacola Bay on November 22 and 23, 1861. After another bombardment by Fort Pickens on January 1 and 2, 1862, Confederates abandoned Pensacola and headed north. In 1865, Fort Barrancas was a Federal base for the Mobile Bay campaign.

The Mississippi District includes Ship Island, used by Admiral David Farragut as a base of operations for attacks on New Orleans and Mobile Bay.

Ft. Massachusetts

Visitors may explore the island and Fort Massachusetts where they can learn about African American soldiers stationed there, and a U.S. military stockade.

Ft. Pickens

Louisiana Native Guards
on Ship Island

One of the earliest African American regiments serving the U.S. Army during the Civil War garrisoned at Ship Island off the coast of Mississippi, which today is part of Gulf Islands National Seashore. Originally known as the 2nd Regiment of Louisiana Native Guards, these former slaves and free people of color were reorganized into the 74th United States Colored Infantry in 1863. On April 9, 1863, the Native Guards experienced their only combat during a successful raid on Pascagoula, Mississippi. Like many United States Colored Troops, the 74th performed mainly manual labor and guard duty.

Between 1862 and 1870, Ship Island's military stockade included thousands of people: civilian political prisoners (including women), Confederate soldiers,

and military convicts. Diseases such as diarrhea, pneumonia, scurvy, typhoid, and dysentery caused the death of 153 prisoners. Between 1863 and 1865, about 260 Union soldiers died from similar causes.

Illustration by Thomas O'Dea,
a former prisoner at Andersonville

Living history
program

Andersonville National Historic Site
began as a stockade built about 14 months
before the end of the Civil War to hold
Union army prisoners captured by Confederate soldiers. Located deep behind
Confederate lines, the 26.5-acre Camp Sumter (named for the south Georgia
county it occupied) was designed for a maximum of 10,000 prisoners. At its most
crowded, it held more than 32,000 men—many of them wounded and starving
—in horrific conditions with rampant disease, contaminated water, and only
minimal shelter from the blazing sun and the chilling winter rain. In the prison's
14 months of existence, some 45,000 Union prisoners arrived here; of those,
12,920 died and were buried in a cemetery created just outside the prison walls.

The cemetery site serving Camp Sumter was designated as Andersonville
National Cemetery on July 26, 1865. By 1868, the burial grounds held the

remains of more than 13,800 Union soldiers whose bodies had been retrieved after their deaths in hospitals, battles, or prison camps throughout the region. Andersonville National Cemetery has been used continuously since its founding and currently averages 130 to 150 burials a year. The cemetery and associated prison site became a unit of the National Park Service in 1970.

Today, Andersonville National Historic Site comprises three distinct components: the former prison site of Camp Sumter, Andersonville National Cemetery, and the National Prisoner of War Museum, which opened in 1998 to honor all U.S. prisoners of war.

Georgia

CHICKAMAUGA AND CHATTANOOGA NATIONAL MILITARY PARK

P.O. Box 2128 • Fort Oglethorpe, GA 30742 • 706-866-9241
(also located in Tennessee)

In late summer and fall of 1863, the Union Army of the Cumberland and the Confederate Army of Tennessee found themselves locked in a desperate struggle for the city of Chattanooga, known as the "Gateway to the Deep South." In efforts to gain control of the city, the armies fought two major battles during a nine-week period, with each side claiming a victory.

On September 18, 1863, Confederate Gen. Braxton Bragg attempted to wedge his troops between the Union army and Chattanooga. Fighting began along West Chickamauga Creek and did not cease until after dark. Early on September 19, Union infantry engaged Confederate cavalry near Jay's Mill, beginning a fight that eventually spread almost four miles. By the end of the day, the Confederates pushed the Union troops back to the LaFayette Road. The next morning, September 20, Confederates again tried to wedge themselves between the Union army and Chattanooga. This move was failing until a gap accidentally opened in the Union line, at which time Confederates happened to launch an assault, pouring through the gap and routing most of the Union army. However, some troops managed to rally and to form a new battle line on Horseshoe Ridge. Union forces held off numerous attacks against the ridge but ultimately retreated to Chattanooga. The Battle of Chickamauga was a Confederate victory and the second bloodiest

Snodgrass Cabin

Union headquarters in Chattanooga

Point Park Gate

Lookout Mountain

battle of the Civil War, yielding over 34,000 casualties.

On November 23, 1863, after a two-month siege, Union forces under the command of Maj. Gen. Ulysses S. Grant struck Confederate forces at Orchard Knob, forcing the small Confederate force there to retreat to the Confederate main line of defense. The next day, November 24, Union troops scaled, assaulted, and took Lookout Mountain. Finally, on November 25, the center of the Confederate line on Missionary Ridge was pierced, sending the gray-clad soldiers reeling back into north Georgia. By winning the decisive Battles for Chattanooga, the gateway opened for the Union's lethal thrust toward the military industrial heart of the Deep South in 1864.

In 1890, two decades after the war, President Benjamin Harrison signed into law the act creating Chickamauga and Chattanooga National Military Park. Today, the nation's first national military park preserves over 9,000 acres of historic ground for visitors to explore and study.

The battle for Fort Pulaski was an important part of the long-range Union strategy to blockade the Confederate coastline and its ports. Fought early in the war in April 1862, the two-day battle produced important results. The fort was surrendered by the Confederate troops inside, which gave the Union forces control of the entrance to the Savannah River. This allowed the Federals to close the port of Savannah to trade. Savannah had been an important port for exporting cotton and importing weapons. By the end of 1862, only a few Confederate ports remained open for blockade runners to bring in vital supplies to the South. The Union kept Savannah closed for the rest of the war.

The Union achieved its quick victory at Fort Pulaski with the help of new technology—rifled cannons. The new type of cannons were far more powerful and effective than the older style smoothbore cannons. The new artillery was so good that the battle at Fort Pulaski made brick and stone forts obsolete. Up until the Civil War, the nation defended its coastline with brick forts. The advance of rifled technology forced the country—and the rest of the world—to find a replacement for the brick forts.

Although Fort Pulaski witnessed only one battle in its history, the fort's story is one that reaches beyond the Civil War. It is a story that spans time and

Union soldiers at Ft. Pulaski, 1863

cultures—a story of people lulled into a false sense of security while new technology quietly advances to undermine their safety. The Confederates inside the fort were comforted by traditional wisdom and a personal reassurance from Gen. Robert E. Lee that they were holding an invincible position. The surprising surrender of the fort in less than two days showed the dramatic impact of new technology and highlighted a universal human lesson, never underestimate your adversary.

In the spring of 1864, Gen. Ulysses S. Grant's orders to Gen. William T. Sherman were to attack the Confederate army in Georgia, "break it up, and go into the interior of the enemy's country as far as you can, inflicting all the damage you can upon their war resources." Following these orders, Sherman attacked the Confederate Army of Tennessee under Gen. Joseph E. Johnston driving it back toward Atlanta through May and into June. By June 19, Johnston's forces were entrenched in a strong defensive position anchored on Kennesaw Mountain and blocking most of the available roadways Sherman would need to continue his advance. After an attempt to flank Johnston's position was blocked by a Confederate counterattack on June 22, Sherman made the decision to make a frontal assault on the Confederate position. Sherman ordered Generals George Thomas and James McPherson to make attacks on the Confederate line on June 27. McPherson attacked with three brigades astride the Burnt Hickory Road. Deadly fire from the entrenched Confederates drove the attacking forces to ground and the attack was soon called off.

Meanwhile, south of the Dallas Road, 8,000 Union infantrymen in five of General Thomas's brigades unsuccessfully attacked the two best divisions in Johnston's army, commanded by Generals Patrick R. Cleburne and Benjamin Franklin Cheatham.

Although both frontal assaults were unsuccessful, a diversionary movement by forces under Union Gen. John Schofield was successful in seizing an important road junction that placed Union forces closer to the Chattahoochee River crossings than Johnston's army. Exploiting this success, Sherman began to shift his troops forcing Johnston to evacuate the Kennesaw line on July 2.

Kolb House

Union General Sherman outside Atlanta

By mid-July, the Confederate forces had retreated to the fortifications of Atlanta where, through the rest of July and all of August, a series of battles were fought which ultimately forced the Confederate army under the command of Gen. John Bell Hood to evacuate the city. The conclusion of the Atlanta campaign, a Union success, was one of the important factors in insuring the reelection of Abraham Lincoln in 1864.

LINCOLN HOME NATIONAL HISTORIC SITE

413 South Eighth Street • Springfield, IL 62701 • 217-492-4241

Many of Abraham Lincoln's social and political beliefs were formed long before he arrived in Washington, D.C. Indeed, many of his beliefs on democracy and freedom were nurtured and developed while he lived at the corner of Eighth and Jackson streets in Springfield, Illinois. Abraham Lincoln came of age while living and working as a private citizen in Springfield. It was here that he built a life for himself and his family, and worked hard to achieve success.

Today, Lincoln Home National Historic Site, under the guidance of the National Park Service, preserves the only home ever owned by Abraham Lincoln. The Lincoln home is the centerpiece of a restored four-block neighborhood containing 12 historic structures dating back to Lincoln's time.

Restored to its 1860 appearance, the home reveals Lincoln as husband, father, neighbor, and president-elect, as well as a man who experienced the same hopes, dreams, and challenges of life still experienced by people today. Ranger-led tours of the home focus on the Lincoln family, Lincoln's rise as a successful lawyer and politician, along with his 1860 presidential campaign.

Lincoln Boyhood National Memorial

2916 East South Street • Lincoln City, IN 47552 • 812-937-4541

Lincoln Living Historical Farm

Cabin Site Memorial

Lincoln Boyhood National Memorial preserves the site of the farm where Abraham Lincoln spent 14 formative years of his life, from the ages of seven to 21. He and his family moved to Indiana in 1816 and stayed until 1830, when they moved on to Illinois. During this period, Lincoln grew physically and intellectually into a man. The people he knew here and the things he experienced had a profound influence on his life. His sense of honesty, his belief in the importance of education and learning, his respect for hard work, his compassion for his fellow man, and his moral convictions about right and wrong were all born of this place and this time. The time he spent here helped shape the man who went on to lead the country. This site is our most direct tie with that time of his life. Lincoln Boyhood preserves the place where he learned to laugh with his father, cried over the death of his mother, read the books that opened his mind, and triumphed over the adversities of life on the frontier.

Fort Larned National Historic Site

1767 KS Highway 156 • Larned, KS 67550 • 620-285-6911

Ft. Larned, 1867

Established along the Pawnee Fork on October 22, 1859, Fort Larned was one of several military posts maintained by the U.S. Army to protect mail transports and commercial trade along the Santa Fe Trail. The fort was staffed with regular army troops until the start of the Civil War. When these men were transferred to join Union forces in the East, volunteer units from Colorado, Wisconsin, and Kansas made up the garrison. Serving at Fort Larned were "Galvanized Yankees," Confederate war prisoners who agreed to join the Union army in return for their release.

During the Civil War, soldiers at Fort Larned carried out their protection and escort duties. The fort's first stone structure, the Blockhouse, was constructed in June 1864 after a Kiowa war party raided the fort, stealing most of the garrison's horses and mules.

The Civil War period coincides with the peak interpretive period of the completely restored and furnished Fort Larned. Visitors learn about garrison life and weapons of the Civil War. A reproduction dugout is used as an example of soldiers' Civil War era accommodations at the fort. The interpretive center provides information about the Civil War and its impact on Fort Larned and the western United States.

P.O. Box 918 • Old Fort Boulevard • Fort Scott, KS 66701 • 620-223-0310

Living history encampment

Capt. George McCoon, 3rd WI Infantry

On the heels of the turbulent "Bleeding Kansas" era in the late 1850s, lingered the specter of civil war. By 1861, the frontier military post of Fort Scott had been abandoned for over eight years and a territorial town of the same name had grown in its place. With war, the U.S. Army returned, this time to the new state of Kansas, and established a headquarters at Fort Scott. When the Kansas-Nebraska Act opened the area to settlement, tensions mounted as abolitionist, free state, and pro-slavery factions flooded into the territory. By mid-1857, the army deployed to the area and engaged in suppressing guerilla activity. Following the Marais des Cygnes massacre, the territorial governor held a "peace conference" at Fort Scott.

During the Civil War, Fort Scott became a major supply, recruitment, and training depot. It included an Army general hospital, an original national cemetery, a small military prison, and served as refuge for thousands displaced by war. The 1864 Battle of Mine Creek to the north was one of the largest cavalry actions of the war. By October 1865, the military presence was gone, only to reappear in 1869 to protect railroad workers from angry settlers.

Nicodemus, ca. 1880

Established in 1877 by former enslaved African Americans, Nicodemus is the oldest and only remaining all-black town west of the Mississippi River. The first settlers left Kentucky in organized colonies at the end of the post-Civil War Reconstruction period to experience freedom on the free soils of Kansas. Like their white counterparts elsewhere on the frontier, they lived in primitive conditions. Newcomers were shaken by the spectacle of homes dug into the ground. By the mid 1880s, hard-working, strong-willed settlers transformed Nicodemus into a prosperous town. When the railroad line failed to reach Nicodemus, the town began a gradual decline. Today, about 25 people live in Nicodemus, most direct descendants of the early settlers. The site is administered by the National Park Service and is comprised of five structures: the St. Francis Hotel/Fletcher-Switzer residence, the Old First Baptist Church, the African Methodist Episcopal (AME) Church, Nicodemus District Number 1 School, and the Township Hall. The Township Hall is the only historic building presently open to the public.

2995 Lincoln Farm Road · Hodgenville, KY 42748 · 270-358-3137

Knob Creek Farm

Abraham Lincoln Birthplace National Historical Park focuses on Abraham Lincoln's life in Kentucky. The park tells the story of our 16th president's humble birth and early life. The park features two units. The Birthplace Unit includes Thomas Lincoln's Sinking Spring Farm. The early 19th-century Kentucky cabin, symbolizing the one in which Abraham was born on February 12, 1809, is enshrined inside the Memorial Building at the site of his birth. The unit also includes the Sinking Spring, site of the Boundary Oak tree. Due to a land dispute, Thomas Lincoln moved his family 10 miles northeast to a farm along Knob Creek. The Knob Creek Boyhood Unit is where the Lincoln family lived on 30 rented acres from the time Abraham was two until he was almost eight years old. As president, he said he could remember planting pumpkin seeds in every other hill and in every other row while others were planting corn. He could remember how he stayed by his mother's side and watched her face while listening to her read the Bible. It was also at Knob Creek that Abraham first saw African Americans being taken south along the Louisville and Nashville Turnpike to be sold as slaves.

CUMBERLAND GAP
NATIONAL HISTORICAL PARK

91 Bartlett Park Road • Middlesboro, KY 40965 • 606-248-2817

When 11 states broke their ties with the U.S. government in spring 1861, military commanders north and south of the Appalachian Mountains began to calculate how to use the Cumberland Gap, located where the states of Virginia, Tennessee, and Kentucky meet, to aid their cause. Federal commanders saw the gap as one way to cut the Confederacy in two. The fact that sentiment was strong against secession in East Tennessee and the mountain counties of neighboring states worked in their favor.

Confederate generals saw the gap as a forward defense against Union strikes that might cripple the salt works, mines, and railroads vital to their war effort. Southerners also saw the gap as a route to invade Kentucky and reclaim its resources for the Confederacy.

Both Union and Confederate regiments spent months at a time at the gap, watching and waiting for the enemy's next move. Here a war of nerves pivoted more

Letter written in 1864

on available supplies and flanking movements than on bombardments or bloody assaults. Numerous Civil War field fortifications perched on high places ringing Cumberland Gap. With cannon sited behind rough log walls and earthworks, these small forts could dominate the steep, twisting roads that approached the strategic gap.

Special heritage events at Cumberland Gap offer visitors the opportunity to see the South through the eyes of those often overlooked. They were the slaves who literally kept the home fires burning, skilled at brick making; the women left at home and their important work of cloth-making; the quartermasters and blacksmiths who supplied the army's needs; the farmers whose livelihood was disrupted and sometimes changed forever by the conflict; and finally, the soldiers—Union and Confederate, white and black—and the hardships and triumphs they experienced.

Louisiana

Magnolia slave tenant cabins

Oakland Main House

CANE RIVER CREOLE
NATIONAL HISTORICAL PARK

400 Rapides Drive • Natchitoches, LA 71457 • 318-352-0383

Cane River Creole National Historical Park's two plantations saw nearly 200 years of continuous ownership by the same families, the Prud'hommes of Oakland Plantation and the LeComte/Hertzog family of Magnolia Plantation. Each ran operations that included hundreds of workers—first enslaved and later free. Like the owners, all residents possessed generational ties to the plantation land, and every generation faced its share of challenges.

In 1864, warring armies passed through the Cane River region during the Red River Campaign. To prevent the valuable cotton crop from falling into Union hands, Confederates burned thousands of bales. Both plantations witnessed further destruction following the Battle of Mansfield when Confederate troops forced a Union retreat south. On their way, Union troops burned Oakland's cotton gin and Magnolia's main house.

The communities at Oakland and Magnolia gradually rebuilt, although the plantations never achieved their pre-Civil War economic prominence that had been based on slavery. Cane River's *gens de couleur libres* (free people of color) lost their pre-Civil War status following Reconstruction and the onset of the Jim Crow era. Freedmen, although no longer enslaved, faced the difficulties of new labor systems: sharecropping and tenant farming.

JEAN LAFITTE NATIONAL HISTORICAL PARK AND PRESERVE

Louisiana

419 Decatur Street • New Orleans, LA 70130 • 504-589-3882

Chalmette National Cemetery

Just as Andrew Jackson had done during the War of 1812, the Confederate defenses in Chalmette relied on earthworks running from the Mississippi River to the swamp.

On April 24, 1862, a Federal fleet sailed up the Mississippi River from the Gulf of Mexico. The fleet dodged fire from forts along the river and collisions with abandoned ships, drifting downriver from New Orleans with cotton cargoes ablaze. As the Federals passed Chalmette's earthworks, 32-pound cannon there and on the river's west bank opened fire until their ammunition was gone.

After the capture of New Orleans, the defenses were manned by Federal troops. One soldier wrote home describing the nearby half-finished monument to the men of the 1815 Battle of New Orleans. The site became a refugee camp for slaves freed by advancing Federal forces, a burial ground for former slaves and troops from both sides, and finally a national cemetery. After the war, freed slaves established Fazendeville just upriver. The earthworks, a nearby powder magazine, and the village are now gone, contained within Chalmette National Cemetery and Chalmette Battlefield. Though the site's main focus is the Battle of New Orleans, its Civil War history is shared through battlefield visitor center interactives and interpretation at the national cemetery.

ANTIETAM NATIONAL BATTLEFIELD

P.O. Box 158 • Sharpsburg, MD 21782 • 301-432-5124

Antietam National Battlefield is the site of the bloodiest one-day battle in American history. The battle, fought September 17, 1862, between Confederate Gen. Robert E. Lee's Army of Northern Virginia and Union Gen. George B. McClellan's Army of the Potomac, was the culmination of Lee's first invasion of the North. For 12 hours, the opposing forces fought over the countryside along Antietam Creek and around the small town of Sharpsburg, Maryland, immortalizing landmarks such as "The Cornfield," Dunker Church, "Bloody Lane," and Burnside Bridge. At the end of the day, more than 23,000 Americans were killed, wounded, or missing.

The repulse of Confederate forces at Antietam provided President Abraham Lincoln with the impetus to issue the Emancipation Proclamation, an important first step by the United States Government toward ending slavery. Prior to the battle, Lincoln's war objective was to restore the Union. After the battle, the war had a dual purpose—restore the Union and end slavery. As a result, England and France were discouraged from entering the war on behalf of the Confederacy.

An eight-and-one-half-mile driving tour takes visitors through one of the

Dunker Church

Burnside Bridge

Sunken Road

best-preserved battlefields in the United States. At each of the 11 tour stops there are exhibits that provide information to help visitors understand the battle. In addition, there are 101 monuments and more than 300 cast-iron war department tablets that mark this historic ground. The park visitor center has a theater, museum, and museum store. There are two movies shown in the park theater, both explain the Maryland Campaign and the battle. In addition to many other artifacts, the museum features large-scale battle panoramas painted by artist James Hope, an actual participant in the battle. Ranger talks and tours are given on a regular basis, and special programs, such as artillery demonstrations, are held in summer months.

CHESAPEAKE AND OHIO CANAL
NATIONAL HISTORICAL PARK

1850 Dual Highway • Hagerstown, MD 21740 • 301-739-4200

Georgetown replica canal boat

For 74 years, from 1850 to 1924, mule-drawn canal boats carried coal and other cargo from Cumberland, Maryland, to Georgetown along the Chesapeake and Ohio Canal. The canal represents an early effort to develop internal transportation routes that connected the resources of the interior of the country with the factories and markets on the coast. The C&O Canal follows the north shore of the Potomac River. Throughout the war, troops moved across the canal as the Army of the Potomac and the Army of Northern Virginia chased and eluded each other in the Potomac Valley.

During the Civil War, the canal was a supply route for the Union. It was an attractive target for Confederate forces wanting to disrupt the canal's operation, and Union troops were stationed along the canal to defend its works. Confederate units attempted to blow up aqueducts several times. Despite these efforts, none of the major canal structures were seriously damaged, and the canal achieved record shipping totals during the war years. With the Mason-Dixon Line along the northern border of Maryland, the state played a key role as a crossroads in the Underground Railroad. Just as Civil War armies crossed the canal at numerous locations, so too did people escaping enslavement as they headed north.

5801 Oxford Road · Glen Echo, MD 20812 · 301-320-1410

Clara Barton was one of the most famous contributors to Civil War history, and yet she was not a soldier. Nicknamed the "Angel of the Battlefield," she saved countless lives, compassionately stood by those she could not save, searched for missing soldiers, and marked the graves at Andersonville Cemetery. During the Civil War, Miss Barton worked independently. She arranged for donations and carried food, water, and medical supplies directly to the wounded who lay helplessly on the battlefield. She worked during many of the bloodiest battles of the war: 2nd Manassas, Antietam, Fredericksburg, Fort Wagner, the Wilderness, Spotsylvania Court House, and Cold Harbor. Clara Barton brought compassion and hope to the sufferers on both sides but was a staunch supporter of the Union cause. She also supported the needs of African American soldiers and former slaves.

Later in life, she founded and served as first president of the American Red Cross. Clara Barton lived in her Glen Echo, Maryland, home from 1897 until her death in 1912. Now known as Clara Barton National Historic Site, the house was the first national park unit dedicated to the accomplishments of a woman. Visitors can discover Miss Barton's incredible life story as they explore her unusual home on ranger-led tours.

FORT MCHENRY NATIONAL MONUMENT AND HISTORIC SHRINE

End of East Fort Avenue • Baltimore, MD 21230 • 410-962-4290

During the Civil War, Fort McHenry in Baltimore, Maryland, served as a Union transfer prison camp for Southern sympathizers and Confederate prisoners of war. Usually, prisoners were confined at the fort for short periods before being transferred to larger prisons such as Fort Delaware.

In May 1861, Union officials began arresting Marylanders suspected of being Confederate sympathizers. Lincoln suspended the Writ of Habeas Corpus along the military lines from Washington to Philadelphia so many prisoners were never charged with a crime and never received a trial. Those imprisoned came from all classes of civilians and ranks of military. Among them were Baltimore Mayor George William Brown, the city council, the police commissioner, members of the House of Delegates from Baltimore City and County, as well as a congressman and a state senator.

Early in the war, there were 126 prisoners at Fort McHenry. That number grew to 800 in the beginning months of 1863 and, after the Battle of Gettysburg in July 1863, the number of prisoners swelled to 6,957. Then the number of those incarcerated dwindled sharply. By September 1865, there were only four prisoners at the fort. Because of its role as a prison camp during the Civil War, Fort McHenry became known as the "Baltimore Bastille."

535 Hampton Lane • Towson, MD 21286 • 410-823-1309

Former slave Nancy Davis (r) and Eliza Ridgely III

In 1745, Col. Charles Ridgely purchased 1,500 acres of the Northampton tract from a relative of Lord Baltimore. Eventually, the property expanded to 11,000 acres. An ironworks was established on a tributary of the Gunpowder River in Maryland, supplying arms and implements to the Patriot cause during the Revolutionary War. Eventually, Hampton, the Ridgely empire, grew to 25,000 acres with ironworks, grain crops, beef cattle, thoroughbred horses, quarries, mills, and mercantile interests. They employed many types of workers: indentured servants from England and Ireland and also purchased locally; white and black free workers; British prisoners of war; and enslaved African Americans.

While difficult to estimate, the Ridgelys enslaved over 500 people. Governor Ridgely owned approximately 350. In all, 92 people were manumitted at his death. This included men aged 28-45, women aged 25-45, and 17 infants. Slavery was part of the Hampton estate until Maryland State law ended it in 1864. In 1938, John Ridgely, Jr., inherited the core of Hampton property and resided in the mansion with his family. The mansion and 43 acres were designated a national historic site in 1948. John and his wife, Jane, continued to live at Hampton, residing in the lower house until their deaths. In 1979, the National Park Service took over administration of the mansion and 60 acres.

MONOCACY NATIONAL BATTLEFIELD

4801 Urbana Pike • Frederick, MD 21704 • 301-662-3515

By summer 1864, Gen. Robert E. Lee's Confederates had established battle lines near Richmond and Petersburg, Virginia. To strengthen Union forces besieging these cities, Lt. Gen. Ulysses S. Grant shifted thousands of troops from their defense of the forts surrounding the United States capital leaving Washington, D.C., vulnerable and tempting. Lee sent Lt. Gen. Jubal Early with an army of nearly 15,000 men to protect Lynchburg, Virginia, and secure the Shenandoah Valley from Union invaders under Gen. David Hunter. After driving Hunter toward the Kanawha Valley, Early made the decision to continue into Maryland, threaten Washington, D.C., and perhaps capture the Federal capital.

Early's army reached Harpers Ferry, West Virginia, on July 4, then crossed the Potomac River into Maryland. Railroad agents alerted Baltimore and Ohio Railroad President John W. Garrett of the approaching forces. Garrett requested protection from Union Maj. Gen. Lew Wallace.

On the morning of July 9, 1864, Early and his army converged on Frederick, Maryland. Three miles south, at Monocacy Junction, Union Gen. Lew Wallace waited with a force of 6,600 men consisting of untested 100-days men, three-year volunteers with limited experience, and veterans who had just arrived from Petersburg. Although outnumbered, Wallace hoped to delay Early until reinforcements arrived in Washington.

Period engraving of the grounds

Worthington House

At roughly 8:30 a.m., Confederates engaged their opponents at the junction and reconnoitered. The Union position was well defended, so an alternate means was needed to cross Monocacy River. Confederate cavalrymen forded downstream from the junction near Worthington Farm. They dismounted and attacked twice, failing to dislodge the well-protected Union defenders, before being forced to fall back.

By late afternoon, Confederate infantry attacked in echelon. With the aid of artillery, they successfully forced Wallace back, creating a gap between the river and flank. Early drove through, forcing Wallace to withdraw from the battlefield and return to Baltimore. The Confederates won their only undisputed victory in the North, but lost a precious day in their march on Washington. Their loss allowed time for reinforcements to arrive in Washington and helped secure Lincoln's opportunity for reelection.

Monocacy National Battlefield's visitor center, trails, and self-guided auto tour are open daily except for Thanksgiving, Christmas, and New Year's.

Use this page for cancellations or field notes.

Charles Francis Adams, Jr.

John and Abigail Adams opposed slavery. John and other founding fathers hoped slavery would end naturally, however, it was left to the next generation. Three subsequent generations of Adamses continued the family tradition of public service. After his presidency, John Quincy Adams was elected to the House of Representatives where he opposed slavery from 1831 until his death in 1848. In 1841, he successfully defended the Mendi people in the Amistad case before the Supreme Court. John Quincy Adams's wife, Louisa, also supported abolition. She assisted her husband by organizing the thousands of anti-slavery petitions he received while fighting to have them recognized in Congress. Their son, Charles Francis Adams, was appointed by President Lincoln to serve as minister plenipotentiary to Great Britain during the Civil War. He is credited with maintaining British neutrality. Two of the ambassador's sons also served the war effort. Charles Francis Adams, Jr., served as a colonel in the Union army, and Henry Adams served as his father's secretary in London and as a correspondent for a New York newspaper. From diplomatic relations to the battlefield, John and Abigail Adams' descendants made important contributions to end slavery and preserve the Union.

Portrait of John Quincy Adams by Edward Marchant, 1840

Robert Gould Shaw Memorial

Boston African American NHS works together with the Museum of African American History to preserve and interpret the inspiring history of the free black community in antebellum Boston. Living on Beacon Hill, this community, along with its white allies, led the nation in the struggle to abolish slavery. The primary way to experience this site is by taking a ranger-guided tour of the Black Heritage Trail. While much of the tour focuses on the abolition movement, there are strong connections to the Civil War with several sites along the trail. The African Meeting House was used as a recruitment center for the 54th Regiment, the first black regiment raised in the North. Recruiting for the 54th across the northeast, Frederick Douglass urged, "Men of Color, To Arms!" Through their bravery and sacrifice at the Battle of Fort Wagner, the 54th Regiment helped to erode northern public opposition to black soldiers and paved the way for close to 200,000 African Americans fighting on the side of the North. Sitting atop Beacon Hill since 1897, Augustus Saint-Gaudens's artistic masterpiece, the Robert Gould Shaw Memorial, commemorates the brave 54th and serves as a powerful reminder of the costs of war and freedom.

BOSTON HARBOR ISLANDS
NATIONAL RECREATION AREA

Massachusetts

408 Atlantic Avenue, Suite. 228 • Boston, MA 02110 • 617-223-8666

Ft. Warren gunners

Many of the 160,000 Massachusetts troops who served the Union during the Civil War shipped to the South through the islands of Boston Harbor, now Boston Harbor Islands National Recreation Area. One island, Georges Island, is home to Fort Warren. Fort Warren served two principal functions during the war. It was a training camp for Union troops and a depot for Confederate prisoners. Prisoners were treated in a respectful manner that was atypical during the Civil War. Of more than 2,000 prisoners, there were only 13 fatalities—all caused by disease. Notable prisoners held at the fort included Vice President of the Confederacy Alexander Stephens, Confederate Postmaster-General John Regan, members of the Maryland legislature, and Confederate commissioners John Mason and James Slidell—captured during the Trent Affair. Among the Massachusetts troops were individuals from the African American, Irish American, and Native American communities. Through their service, they proved their loyalty to the nation. Join us in commemorating the Civil War by visiting Boston Harbor Islands. Learn the history of coastal fortifications in Boston Harbor at the Georges Island Visitor Center. Participate in special events. Walk Fort Warren. Talk with park rangers. Experience your America.

Marine guard at Charlestown Navy Yard, ca. 1874

Boston National Historical Park's connection to the American Civil War is both political and military. Sites such as the Old South Meeting House and Faneuil Hall were just two of the sites used by abolitionists, such as Frederick Douglass and William Lloyd Garrison to speak about the evils of slavery. Once the war broke out, these two sites were used as recruiting stations or rallying sites for the tens of thousands of soldiers needed to preserve the Union. In fact, Faneuil Hall was even used as a barracks for the early three-month regiments sent to Washington, D.C.

The most prominent site in Boston that is connected to the American Civil War is the Navy Yard in Charlestown, Massachusetts. It was here that many of the ships used to blockade the South and to support land operations were built or refitted. Most notable of these ships were USS *Hartford*, USS *Housatonic* and USS *Cumberland*. It was also here that the infamous Confederate Ironclad CSS *Virginia* began its service in the U.S. Navy as the USS *Merrimack*.

105 Brattle Street • Cambridge, MA 02138 • 617-876-4491

Longfellow House, ca. 1863

Longfellow House—Washington's Headquarters NHS preserves the home of Henry Wadsworth Longfellow, one of the world's foremost 19th-century poets. The house also served as headquarters for General George Washington during the Siege of Boston, July 1775 to April 1776. In addition to its rich history, the site offers unique opportunities to explore 19th-century literature and arts. The site has a number of artifacts and archives, and many stories to tell about the Civil War. Henry Longfellow was a staunch abolitionist and wrote *Poems On Slavery* in 1842 and *Paul Revere's Ride* in 1860, a bold statement of his opposition to slavery. He made many monetary contributions to free slaves, and to support African Americans and their schools and churches. He was friends with Charles Sumner —the abolitionist senator from Massachusetts who was attacked in the senate because of his scathing speech against slavery—and supported his causes. Furthermore, his son, Charles Appleton Longfellow, joined the Union army and was badly wounded at the Battle of New Hope Church. Charley's uniform, weapons, journals, correspondence, photographs, books and other materials from his period of service, as well as his life after discharge from the army, are preserved at the site. The site also holds papers of the Dana family, including Richard Henry Dana, Jr.'s legal records used during his defense of slave rescuers due to the 1850 Fugitive Slave Act, and the defense of Anthony Burns, a fugitive slave in 1854.

67 Kirk Street • Lowell, MA 01852 • 978-970-5000

Baltimore riots, April 1861

After President Lincoln's call for troops on April 15, the Massachusetts 6th Regiment of Volunteers mustered in what is today Lowell National Historical Park under command of Lowell's Gen. Benjamin F. Butler, and was ordered to Washington, D.C., in defense of the capital. On April 19, the regiment arrived in Baltimore and marched through the streets while being followed in hot pursuit and taunted by Southern sympathizers. Brickbats, rocks, and gunfire flew at the troops, and Colonel Jones ordered his soldiers to fire in defense. When the riots ended, four soldiers from the regiment lay dead in the street: Addison Whitney, Luther Ladd, James Taylor, and Sumner Needham became the first casualties in the Civil War. Lowell NHP interprets the Civil War through curriculum education, ranger-led interpretive programming, and exhibits.

The Pollard Memorial Library (Memorial Hall, 1893) commemorates "those patriotic men who gave their service and lives in the War of the Rebellion 1861-1865." Three impressive Civil War scenes by Paul Philippoteaux, who painted the Gettysburg Cyclorama (1883), grace the second floor reference room. Dramatic Civil War depictions are carved into the exterior granite friezes of the building.

33 William Street • New Bedford, MA 02740 • 508-996-4095

Reenactor scales the rigging

COLORED MEN, ATTENTION!
YOUR COUNTRY CALLS!
One Hundred Colored Men Wanted.
To be attached to
Gov. Andrew's New Regiment,
THE MASSACHUSETTS FIFTY-FOURTH.
The Pay and Rations to be the same as those of any other Massachusetts Regiment. The families of the Colored men enlisting to receive the same as that furnished white men in other Regiments
Head-Quarters for enlisting at the first building west of the Post Office. William street.
N. B.—Colored men from any other town, city, or State, wishing to enlist, will be received the same as though they were from this city.
feb12   J. W. GRACE, Recruiting Officer,

Few cities in the North contributed more to the Union than did New Bedford. In men, goods, supplies, and funds, people who had made their fortunes in New Bedford through whaling poured what they could into the war effort. In 1863, New Bedford became the recruiting grounds for Company C of the Massachusetts 54th Regiment. The 54th was the first regiment of "colored" men organized within the Union army. New Bedford's William Carney, a sergeant in the 54th, was the first African American to earn the Medal of Honor. Despite being wounded three times, Carney never let the U.S. flag touch the ground at the Battle of Fort Wagner. The 54th went on to distinguish itself in the course of the war. But New Bedford provided more than just manpower. When the U.S. Navy was searching for ships to sink in Southern ports in an attempt to make a blockade, New Bedford answered the call. As the "Great Stone Fleet" disappeared beneath the waves of Charleston Harbor, captains watched as New Bedford ships plunged out of sight. Throughout the war, New Bedford supported its troops in the field with food, clothes, and donations. The city sacrificed the lives of its men and ships to the Union cause.

SPRINGFIELD ARMORY
NATIONAL HISTORIC SITE

1 Armory Square • Springfield, MA 01105 • 413-734-8551

With the destruction of Harpers Ferry Armory on April 18, 1861, the Union turned to Springfield Armory, the sole surviving government armory, for rifle production. Springfield Armory accelerated production of percussion rifle muskets after the first 15 months of war, allowing the Ordnance Department to cease depending on private contractors to supplement its needs.

Springfield Armory was among the best managed and productive industrial centers in the nation. Nearly half a century of managerial and technological innovation firmly established what was called "Armory practice." Production of interchangeable and uniform weapons was normal through the application of gages and mechanized machinery, full inspection of parts, and a sophisticated division of labor.

The timing of the successful development of large-scale musket making at Springfield proved most fortunate for the U.S. Army. In 1864 alone, the armory manufactured more than 276,000 rifle muskets. During the course of the war, over 800,000 rifle muskets were produced here. Before the start of the Civil War, Springfield Armory was better known for making first-rate muskets than for designing them. The war changed that as the U.S. Army started looking for a new rifle in 1864. Springfield became the prime military small arms research center for the next century.

Use this page for cancellations or field notes.

Use this page for cancellations or field notes.

BRICES CROSS ROADS NATIONAL BATTLEFIELD SITE

Mississippi

c/o Natchez Trace Parkway
2680 Natchez Trace Parkway • Tupelo, MS 38804 • 662-680-4025

Brices Cross Roads

Brices Cross Roads and Tupelo National Battlefields are one-acre monument sites today, but they each represent important battles that took place in Northeast Mississippi in June and July 1864. They were part of a larger Federal effort during the summer of 1864 to keep Maj. Gen. Nathan B. Forrest and his Confederate horseman in Mississippi and out of east Tennessee and north Georgia. This would ensure that Forrest would not interrupt Maj. Gen. William T. Sherman's critical "March to the Sea" in Georgia. Students of military tactics agree that the Brices Cross Roads engagement marked a brilliant tactical victory for Forrest. An important element of the story at both Brices Cross Roads and the Battle of Tupelo was the role played by the United States Colored Troops (USCT). USCT troops commanded by Col. Edward Bouton played critical roles in both battles. At Brices Cross Roads, the USCT made several critical stands that slowed the Confederate pursuit of the Federal retreat.

Exhibits and information on both battles can be found at the Natchez Trace Parkway Visitor Center in Tupelo.

Slave cabin interior

Natchez National Historical Park operates two separate sites within Natchez: the William Johnson House and the Melrose Estate, home of wealthy planter John T. McMurran. However, the boundaries of interpretation extend throughout the city, as the park exists to help tell the story of all the people of Natchez from colonial times to present day.

Before the Civil War in Natchez, wealthy planters such as John T. McMurran were living in elaborate city homes like Melrose. Slaves living and working on the plantations afforded planters the wealth of such homes. Between 1833 and the Civil War, the slave market in Natchez, known as Forks of the Road, grew into the second largest slave market in the Deep South, second only to New Orleans.

During the Civil War in 1863, Union forces occupied Natchez and ended slavery and slave trading in the city. Some plantation slaves ran from enslavement to areas like Natchez, not only seeking protection with the Union army but to join the Union army to fight for their own freedom. Many of the planter class in Natchez were Union sympathizers while their sons joined to fight for the Confederate army.

2680 Natchez Trace Parkway • Tupelo, MS 38804 • 662-680-4025

Mount Locust

The Natchez Trace Parkway commemorates the historic travel route from Natchez, Mississippi, to Nashville, Tennessee. Heavily used by the boatmen of the Ohio River Valley in the late 1700s and early 1800s, this land travel route provided a direct route home for the "Kaintucks" after they sold their goods in Natchez. Built in 1779, Mount Locust is the oldest surviving stand along the parkway. It grew from a small corn farm to a thriving cotton plantation. The 1820 census lists 26 enslaved people at Mount Locust, and by the middle of the 19th century, that number had reached 51. Archeologists believe 12 to 16 slave cabins once stood on the property, with four to five people occupying each dwelling. On the west side of Mount Locust, a cemetery holds the remains of 43 enslaved workers.

Much of the Natchez Trace had been abandoned for years when the Civil War began. A significant section of Old Trace, known as the Old Port Gibson Road survived and was used heavily by Gen. Ulysses S. Grant during his 1863 Vicksburg campaign. Along the Natchez Trace Parkway there are Civil War sites at Port Gibson, the Dillon Plantation site (adjacent to Dean Stand site, milepost 73.5) and the Battle of Raymond site (milepost 78.3).

Mississippi

VICKSBURG NATIONAL MILITARY PARK

3201 Clay Street • Vicksburg, MS 39183 • 601-636-0583

Situated midway between Memphis and New Orleans on bluffs that tower 300 feet above the Mississippi River, Vicksburg was a powerful Confederate bastion that mounted 172 cannon. In addition to the city's formidable river batteries, nine forts connected by rifle-pits guarded all land approaches to Vicksburg. Manned by a garrison of 30,000 troops commanded by Lt. Gen. John C. Pemberton, the city was known as the "Gibraltar of America." "Vicksburg is the key," said President Abraham Lincoln who realized "that the war can never be brought to a close until that key is in our pocket." In equally powerful language, Confederate President Jefferson Davis declared Vicksburg to be the "nail head that held the South's two halves together." Thus the campaign waged for control of Vicksburg and the great river proved to be the most decisive of the Civil War.

In spring 1863, Maj. Gen. Ulysses S. Grant launched his Union Army of the Tennessee on a bold campaign to

Union Avenue

Contemporary lithograph of Siege at Vicksburg

Illinois Monument

USS *Cairo*

pocket that key. After crossing the river below Vicksburg, Grant's army pushed deep into the interior of Mississippi and captured Jackson, the state capital. Turning west, the Union army battled its way to Vicksburg and drove Confederate forces into the city's defenses. After two failed assaults, the campaign culminated in a 47-day siege of the city that surrendered on July 4, 1863. President Lincoln sighed, "Thank God. The Father of Waters again flows unvexed to the sea."

Vicksburg National Military Park encompasses approximately 1,800 acres and includes the grounds of Vicksburg National Cemetery—the final resting place of 17,000 Union soldiers and sailors. The park also features the restored ironclad gunboat USS *Cairo* and USS *Cairo* Museum, the remaining vestige of Grant's canal, and Pemberton's headquarters in the heart of Vicksburg where the decision was made to surrender the city.

During the Civil War, guerilla warfare intensified along the Missouri-Kansas border. Born enslaved on a farm owned by Moses and Susan Carver, George Washington Carver was caught in the turmoil. When Carver was an infant, outlaws kidnapped him and his mother, Mary. A very ill George was found in Arkansas and was returned to the Carvers. His mother, tragically, was never found. Carver spent much of his childhood on this southwest Missouri farm. These years stoked his desire for learning and shaped his values. Carver eventually reached acclaim as a scientist, teacher, and humanitarian while employed at Tuskegee Institute where he spent the last 47 years of his life. His innovative farming methods, dedication to alleviating poverty, and calls for interracial cooperation, inspired thousands. In Carver's words, he dedicated himself "to be the greatest good to the greatest number of my people." In 1943, Carver's birthplace became the first national park dedicated to an African American when Congress designated George Washington Carver National Monument six months after he died. The park preserves all 240 acres of the original Carver farm, and interprets the struggles, triumphs, and profound legacy of George Washington Carver.

Harriet and Dred Scott

Old Courthouse

One of the major contributing factors that led to the Civil War involved a humble, enslaved man named Dred Scott and his suit for freedom. Scott's famous case was launched in St. Louis's Old Courthouse in 1846, which today is preserved as part of Jefferson NEM. Scott and his wife, Harriet, sued for their freedom because they had been taken to free territories by their enslaver. The Scotts lost their first trial in 1847. At a second trial in 1850, a jury decided that they should be free. The case was appealed to the Missouri Supreme Court, which reversed the ruling. Scott was not ready to give up his fight for freedom, and filed suit in federal court in 1854. Although he lost, Scott appealed to the U.S. Supreme Court. On March 6, 1857, Chief Justice Roger B. Taney delivered the majority opinion of the court. He also ruled that as a slave, Dred Scott was not a citizen of the United States, and therefore had no right to bring suit in federal courts. In addition, he declared that the federal government had no right to prohibit slavery in the new territories. The court appeared to be saying that slavery could not be outlawed or restricted within the United States. Antislavery groups feared that slavery would now spread unchecked. The new Republican Party's political campaign of 1860, coupled with divisive issues that split the Democratic Party, led to the election of Abraham Lincoln as president and South Carolina's secession from the Union. The Dred Scott decision moved the country to the brink of civil war.

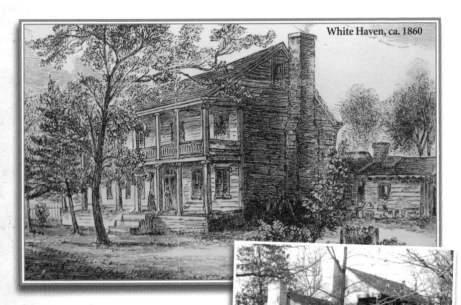

White Haven, ca. 1860

Ulysses S. Grant NHS commemorates the personal and public life of one of the most famous Americans of the 19th century, the general who led the Union armies to victory and the 18th president of the United States. As general, Grant achieved military success fighting for the dual war aims of union and emancipation. As president, he gained political success with his support of the 15th Amendment and civil rights for all Americans. Ulysses S. Grant first visited White Haven, the historic name of the property, in 1843, after graduating from the U.S. Military Academy at West Point, New York. His former roommate, Fred Dent, invited Grant to visit his family, and soon the 22-year-old Ulysses fell in love with Fred's younger sister, Julia. Their marriage on August 22, 1848, would be the beginning of a long and loving partnership that would sustain them both through fame, success, and misfortune. The site provides opportunities to learn about Ulysses and Julia Grant as ordinary individuals facing the joys and challenges of life, as well as people who played significant roles in our nation's history.

Missouri

6424 West Farm Road 182 • Republic, MO 65738 • 417-732-2662

Ray House

Most people believe that the Civil War started in 1861, but in Missouri the war began in 1854 with the passage of the Kansas-Nebraska Act. Border warfare ran rampant between Missouri and Kansas, and the Civil War became the legal excuse people needed to harass and kill their neighbors. Union General Nathaniel Lyon was stationed in St. Louis and was determined to keep Missouri in the Union. Lyon forced pro-Southern Governor Claiborne Jackson, his commanding general Sterling Price, and the beginnings of the state militia to flee to the southwest corner of the state. The two forces met on August 10, 1861, at the Battle of Wilson's Creek.

At the urging of his staff, Lyon split his small force and sent 1,200 men under Colonel Franz Sigel to flank the Confederate right from the south. The main force, directly under Lyon's leadership, took the high ground or what became known as Bloody Hill. Sigel advanced and drove the Confederate forces before him, eventually blocking the Wire Road, which was the Confederate line of retreat. Sigel was set to flight and Lyon faced the entire Confederate army on

Continued

Reenactors portray members of the Missouri State Guard

Bloody Hill. Lyon was mortally wounded leading a charge, and after six hours of fighting, the Union army retreated to Springfield. Lyon became the first Union general killed in combat during the Civil War.

Today, Wilson's Creek National Battlefield consists of 2,000 acres, a modern visitor center with a new interpretive film, a research library, the largest collection of Trans-Mississippi artifacts in the National Park Service, and a five-mile self-guided driving tour with eight stops along the route. Those stops include the Ray House, which served as a hospital, and Bloody Hill. The park offers interpretive programs during the summer months, including artillery and musket firings.

Nathaniel Lyon

8523 West State Highway 4 • Beatrice, NE 68310 • 402-223-3514

The Homestead Act was signed by President Abraham Lincoln on May 20, 1862. The battle over public lands in the West had been a point of contention for Congress for decades. The North wanted to give the land away as small farms to be cultivated. The South opposed this, knowing that small farms were not conducive to slave labor. They feared more free states would form from this arrangement. Southerners also feared a mass exodus of whites to the West in search of opportunity. When the Southern states seceded from the U.S., the South's congressional representation went with them. The Homestead Act was passed because the opposition was absent.

Daniel Freeman and family

Women homesteaders

The Homestead Act ensured that the North would populate the West with Union sympathizers. During the early years of the Civil War, the North feared that a victorious South would take their institutional slavery into the western territories. The Homestead Act guarded against this by allowing only individuals who had "never borne arms against the Government of the United States or given aid and comfort to its enemies" to claim the public lands offered.

One of the first amendments to the 1862 Homestead Act was the 1870 Homestead Act for Civil War Veterans which essentially gave land to Civil War veterans who had "remained loyal to the government," without having to meet the 1862 requirements. These measures were designed to ensure Northern ideals were carried westward and that the evils of institutional slavery would never follow the expansion of the nation.

SAINT-GAUDENS NATIONAL HISTORIC SITE

New Hampshire   139 Saint-Gaudens Road • Cornish, NH 03745 • 603-675-2175

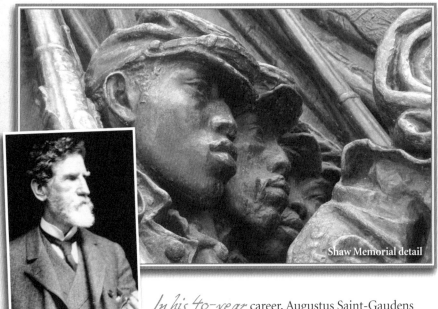

Shaw Memorial detail

In his 40-year career, Augustus Saint-Gaudens (1848-1907) created iconic images of Union leaders of the Civil War. Portraits of Abraham Lincoln, Admiral David Farragut, General William Sherman, General John A. Logan, and the memorial to Colonel Robert Gould Shaw and the Massachusetts 54th Regiment, expressed his passionate obligation to commemorate the sacrifice of those who gave unflinchingly of themselves.

Saint-Gaudens NHS preserves and interprets not only where the sculptor lived and worked, but also contains the largest collection of his work anywhere. Related to the Civil War, the park exhibits two full-scale casts of the Shaw Memorial (a plaster on loan to the National Gallery, Washington, D.C., and a bronze at Cornish), the original stone base of the Farragut Monument with a later bronze cast of the figure, a studio model of the Seated Lincoln, and smaller versions of the Standing Lincoln and Sherman Monument. The park interprets the story of the Shaw Memorial and other themes related to the conflict.

P.O. Box 127 • Waltrous, NM 87753 • 505-425-8025

Aerial view of
the star fort

Fort Union served as the largest supply depot for U.S. outposts throughout the New Mexico Territory from 1851-1891. During the Civil War, the fort was a desired target of the Confederacy. Fort Union was never attacked. However, in March 1862, those who served at Fort Union engaged Confederate forces east of Santa Fe at the battles of Apache Canyon and Glorieta Pass, the turning point of the war in the Southwest. These two battles ended the threat of Confederate domain in New Mexico Territory, and ensured safe travel along the Santa Fe Trail for the Union's Civil War effort.

A notable regiment that participated in the battles of Apache Canyon and Glorieta Pass, was the 1st New Mexico—3rd Regiment Infantry. Organized at Fort Union in 1861, the 1st New Mexico volunteers aided in construction of the earthen fieldwork and played a vital role in the Indian War campaigns. Comprised mostly of Hispanic-American citizens, the volunteers gave and received their orders in Spanish.

Fort Union's second fort, a massive, bastioned earthwork constructed in 1861 and largely abandoned by the close of 1863, stands as an important example of mid-19th-century American military architecture. It is the sole surviving earthen star fort erected west of the Mississippi River and the most intact Civil War-era bastioned earthen fort in the U.S. today.

Battle of Glorieta Pass
painting by Roy Anderson

Living history
demonstration

The Battle of Glorieta Pass is referred to as the "The Gettysburg of the West." In the spring of 1862 along the Santa Fe Trail in New Mexico Territory, Union troops thwarted an ambitious Confederate military campaign designed to expand the Confederacy westward. The Confederates hoped to take control of the mining riches of Colorado and press on to capture key ports in the California Territory.

Much as the Confederates were never again to invade the North after losing the Battle of Gettysburg, they never again attempted significant action in the far West after the Battle of Glorieta Pass. The battle was fought over three days between March 26 and March 28, 1862. Major fighting on the final day was preceded by a lesser and indecisive encounter on March 26.

With approximately 1,200 soldiers on each side, the casualties were high. Union forces suffered 51 killed, 78 wounded, and 15 captured. Among the Confederates, 48 were killed, 80 wounded, and 92 captured. The Battle of Glorieta Pass came more than a year before Gettysburg, and though not anywhere near the magnitude of Gettysburg in terms of men engaged in the fight or resultant casualties, it convincingly demonstrated that the violence of Civil War battles was not confined to the battlefields of the East. The park offers tours of the Battle of Glorieta Pass throughout the year. There is also an interpretive hiking trail.

1960s aerial view of the site

GENERAL GRANT NATIONAL MEMORIAL

122nd Street and Riverside Drive • New York, NY 10027 • 212-666-1640

Period lithograph

General Grant National Memorial in New York pays homage to Ulysses S. Grant, the victorious commanding general of the Union who brought the Civil War to an end. The memorial includes the tombs of General Grant and his wife, Julia Dent Grant. A West Point graduate, Grant served in the Mexican War and at various frontier posts before rising through the ranks during the Civil War. Grant was victorious in the battles of Vicksburg and Chattanooga and accepted Robert E. Lee's surrender at Appomattox. He was respected in both the North and the South. A grateful nation elected him president in 1868 and in 1872. Living in New York City for the last five years of his life, Grant requested to be buried there. He died on July 23, 1885. The granite and marble memorial, which overlooks the Hudson River from Manhattan, was designed by architect John Duncan. It is the largest mausoleum in North America. Grant's Tomb, as it is commonly called, was dedicated on April 27, 1897, with more than one million people in attendance. The memorial is both Grant's final resting place and a tribute to his life.

Castle Williams, ca. 1896

𝒟𝓊𝓇𝒾𝓃ℊ the Civil War, Governors Island in New York Harbor was an important part of the military establishment in New York City. Home to Fort Columbus, now known as Fort Jay, the army post served as a major infantry recruiting center. The island was also home to the U.S. Army's New York Arsenal, supplying pistols, muskets, and artillery from six-pounders to 15-inch Rodman cannon, to army posts along the East Coast. Two fortifications, Fort Columbus and Castle Williams, alternately served as recruit housing and detention facilities for captured Confederate prisoners of war. It was from here that commanding general of the U.S. Army, Winfield Scott, twice called on troops to resupply and reinforce Fort Sumter in Charleston Harbor. On January 5, 1861, 200 troops departed by ship under cover of darkness for Fort Sumter. They were turned back by hostile fire on January 9. President Abraham Lincoln ordered a second attempt, knowing it would likely provoke war, and on April 9, under cover of darkness, the effort was repeated. The departure of the troop barge from Governors Island represented the last tick of the clock before its arrival outside Charleston Harbor prompted the firing on Fort Sumter and the start of the Civil War on April 12, 1861.

Elizabeth Cady Stanton and four Quaker women organized the first public women's rights convention in July 1848, in Seneca Falls, New York. At this convention they advocated political, economic, and social equality for American women. Their personal and professional stories continued through the Civil War. Three of the 1848 Women's Rights Convention organizers—Lucretia Mott, Martha Wright, and Mary Ann M'Clintock—participated in the Underground Railroad. Stanton and M'Clintock helped draft the Declaration of Sentiments, which served as the convention's mission statement.

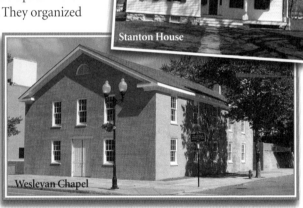

Stanton House

Wesleyan Chapel

The convention organizers used a variety of means to participate in the abolitionist movement. They organized petition drives, presented speeches, and wrote newspaper articles. In 1863, Stanton and Susan B. Anthony formed the Women's National Loyal League, a patriotic organization dedicated to preserving the Union and abolishing slavery. They led a petition drive that demanded the abolition of slavery. This drive formed a grass-roots support for the 13th Amendment.

After the Civil War, Stanton and Anthony advocated the right to vote for former enslaved persons and for all women. Frederick Douglass pressed for a Constitutional amendment that would guarantee the right to vote for African American men. While Stanton and Anthony desired an all-inclusive goal for the right to vote, Douglass favored an incremental approach. Though the goals of preserving the Union and abolishing slavery had been achieved with the end of the Civil War, the struggle for political rights would continue.

8095 Mentor Avenue • Mentor, OH 44060 • 440-255-8722

When the Confederate army attacked Fort Sumter, James A. Garfield was a state senator living in Columbus, Ohio. Rather than enlist, he waited for a commission which came several months later as lieutenant colonel of the 42nd Ohio Volunteer Infantry. In December 1861, newly promoted Colonel Garfield received his orders to advance the 42nd OVI to eastern Kentucky. A regiment of Confederates had been seen advancing northeast to the vicinity of Louisville. Garfield moved his command south, down the Big Sandy River and engaged the Confederates at Paintsville. He succeeded in driving the Confederates backwards to Middle Creek, where he ordered an all-out assault. The battle ended in a draw, however, the Confederates burned their supplies and retreated to Virginia. With his success at Middle Creek, Garfield earned a promotion to brigadier general. A year later, he accepted an offer from Gen. William Rosecrans to be chief of staff for the Army of the Cumberland. At the Battle of Chickamauga, Gen. Garfield rode through enemy fire to reach the left flank commanded by Gen. George Thomas to advise him that the remainder of the Union army had fled. For his bravery on the field, Garfield gained the rank of major general. He left the army in October 1863 to take his place in Congress as a newly elected representative. In 1880, James A. Garfield became the 20th president of the U.S.

1195 Baltimore Pike, Suite 100 • Gettysburg, PA 17325 • 717-334-1124

The Angle

Abraham Lincoln, November 1863

Located 50 miles northwest of Baltimore, the small town of Gettysburg, Pennsylvania, was the site of the largest Civil War battle ever waged in the Western Hemisphere. The Battle of Gettysburg opened on July 1, 1863, and closed two days later with the climactic "Pickett's Charge." It resulted in a Union victory for the Army of the Potomac and successfully turned back the second invasion of the North by Gen. Robert E. Lee's Army of Northern Virginia. Over 51,000 soldiers were killed, wounded, or captured making it the bloodiest battle of the Civil War. It was also a major turning point in the war, often referred to as the "High Water Mark of the Confederacy." It was the last major effort by Lee to take the war out of Virginia into the Northern states.

Concerned citizens preserved portions of the battlefield as a memorial to the Union victory. On February 11, 1895, federal legislation was signed that established Gettysburg National Military Park as a memorial dedicated to the armies that fought that great three-day battle. At first administered by a commission of Civil War veterans, the park was transferred to the National Park Service of the Department of the Interior in 1933. Since that time, Gettysburg has come to be known as the symbol of a war that divided this nation. It also serves as the inspiration for the "new birth of freedom" that President Abraham Lincoln so powerfully spoke of on November 19, 1863, when he delivered his Gettysburg Address on the grounds of the new Soldiers' National Cemetery. Today, the cemetery contains more than 7,000 interments, including over 3,500 from the Civil War, of which 979 are unknown.

McPherson's Ridge

Gettysburg NMP incorporates nearly 6,000 acres, with 26 miles of park roads and over 1,328 monuments, markers, and memorials. Over 300 Civil War-era cannon mounted on cast iron carriages stand where artillery batteries were posted during the battle.

HOPEWELL FURNACE
NATIONAL HISTORIC SITE

2 Mark Bird Lane • Elverson, PA 19520 • 610-582-8773

Furnace demonstration

With the coming of the Civil War, the Hopewell Furnace Company ceased production of the famous Hopewell stove to produce the pig iron needed for the manufacturing of Union weapons. With the furnace running 24 hours a day, seven days a week, the furnace company, ironworkers, and their families enjoyed newfound economic prosperity. However, the war brought hardship to the furnace community. Transportation challenges and the military takeover of the railroads isolated the rural community at Hopewell. On the home front, Hopewell residents worried about friends and relatives on the battlefield. Several furnace workers perished during the war. For some workers, the Civil War illustrated the disparities in American society. African Americans like Isaac Cole desired to join their neighbors and fight for the Union. They may, in fact, have had a special yearning to take up arms, as the abolition of slavery became the focus of the war. Ironically, Federal law prohibited African Americans from serving as soldiers. Finally, in 1863, the Union army organized the United States Colored Troops and accepted African American enrollees. In 1864, at the age of 40, Isaac Cole enlisted in Company H, 32nd Regiment U.S. Colored Troops.

143 South Third Street • Philadelphia, PA 19106 • 215-597-8787

The origins of the conflict between the states dates back to the nation's founding in Philadelphia, where in 1776 and 1787, the Founding Fathers debated and signed the Declaration of Independence and U.S. Constitution inside Independence Hall. Though the words of the founders proclaimed that *"all men are created equal,"* the harsh reality of slavery, and the failure of the founding generation to resolve the issue, virtually guaranteed conflict. During the first half of the 19th century, a series of fragile compromises held the nation together. The end came with the election of Abraham Lincoln in 1860 and the secession of Southern states. In February 1861,

President-elect Lincoln visited Independence Hall as he traveled to his inauguration. Raising a flag above the birthplace of the nation, he expressed hope that conflict might still be averted, but if it could not, he would rather be assassinated than surrender the principles enshrined in the Declaration of Independence. Sadly, war could not be prevented. By war's end, the nation had

experienced what President Lincoln called *"a new birth of freedom."* The Union was saved and slavery abolished. The park includes the Liberty Bell which originally hung in the Pennsylvania State House (Independence Hall). The bell is inscribed with, "Proclaim liberty throughout all the land unto all the inhabitants thereof." It was first used as a symbol of freedom by abolitionists prior to the Civil War.

Use this page for cancellations or field notes.

c/o Fort Sumter National Monument
1214 Middle Street • Sullivan's Island, SC 29482 • 843-881-5516

The 1828 house

Charles Pinckney NHS preserves a 28-acre remnant of founding father Charles Pinckney's plantation, Snee Farm. A delegate from South Carolina, Pinckney was a principal drafter and signer of the U.S. Constitution and spent his life in public service. The park interprets Pinckney's contributions to the Constitution, the development of the early nation, and life on a low-country plantation. An 1828 historic house serves as a museum and visitor center. A half-mile walking trail includes the archeological site of a slave community. Through exhibits and film, the site examines constitutional compromises dealing with slavery and the growing sectionalism in the young nation that led to the Civil War. Living history days during National Park Week and Constitution Week allow for cultural programming on military and domestic life during the late 18th and early 19th century. The site is part of the Gullah-Geechee National Cultural Heritage Corridor that seeks to preserve and interpret the unique local culture of descendants of enslaved Africans.

FORT MOULTRIE

c/o Fort Sumter National Monument
1214 Middle Street • Sullivan's Island, SC 29482 • 843-883-3123

One of the United States' most historic coastal defense sites, Fort Moultrie protected the city of Charleston and its strategically important harbor for more than a century and a half. Located on Sullivan's Island, the original palmetto log fort was built in 1776 to prevent British naval incursions into Charleston Harbor. Under the command of Colonel William Moultrie, a decisive American victory on June 28, 1776, galvanized the patriot cause for independence.

The present brick fort was constructed in 1809 and saw action during the Civil War. On December 26, 1860, six days after South Carolina seceded from the Union, Fort Moultrie's small Federal garrison abandoned the fort, moving to the unfinished but more defendable Fort Sumter. State militia troops occupied Fort Moultrie the next day. Confederate Fort Moultrie participated in the April 12, 1861, firing on Fort Sumter that began the Civil War. Heavily damaged by Federal bombardment beginning in 1863, Fort Moultrie remained in Confederate hands until February 1865. During the late 19th and

Evacuation of Ft. Moultrie

Reenactors dressed in military garb from 1776 to 1945

early 20th centuries, Fort Moultrie underwent numerous changes as improving military and engineering technologies added to the complexities of coastal defense. The fort remained an active military installation until it was decommissioned in 1947.

From the site of the palmetto log fort to the defensive structures of World War II, Fort Moultrie's weapons and fortifications reflect the changes that evolved during the nearly 200 years when coastal forts stood as ready sentinels protecting our nation. Fort Moultrie is a unit of Fort Sumter National Monument. Most of its impressive artillery collection dates to the Civil War. An exhibit on the international slave trade deals with Sullivan's Island and Charleston as a main port of entry for captive Africans and slavery as the foundation of South Carolina's antebellum plantation society.

South Carolina

FORT SUMTER NATIONAL MONUMENT

1214 Middle Street • Sullivan's Island, SC 29482 • 843-883-3123

When the Civil War finally exploded in Charleston Harbor, it was the result of a half-century of growing sectionalism. Escalating crises over property rights, human rights, states rights, and constitutional rights divided the country as it expanded westward. Underlying all the economic, social, and political rhetoric was the volatile question of slavery. Because its economic life had long depended on enslaved labor, South Carolina was the first state to secede when this way of life was threatened. Confederate forces fired the first shot in South Carolina, and the Federal government responded with force. Decades of compromise were over, and the very nature of the Union was at stake.

Fort Sumter National Monument commemorates the beginning of the Civil War on April 12, 1861, when Confederate artillery opened fire on this Federal fort in Charleston Harbor. Fort Sumter surrendered 34 hours

later, and a divided country entered the refining fire of four years of bloody conflict. Confederate-occupied Fort Sumter was a highly symbolic target for Union guns during the 18-month Siege of Charleston.

Today a stabilized ruin, its walls tell the story of destruction to visitors year round. Museum exhibits, ranger talks, and living history programs help visitors connect to this transformative period in U.S. history. The Civil War not only led to the end of slavery, but it also redefined citizenship and strengthened the role of the Federal government in protecting this "new birth of freedom."

Fort Sumter is accessible by private boat or concessionaire ferry. Hours vary seasonally.

Use this page for cancellations or field notes.

ANDREW JOHNSON NATIONAL HISTORIC SITE

Tennessee

121 Monument Avenue • Greeneville, TN 37743 • 423-639-3711

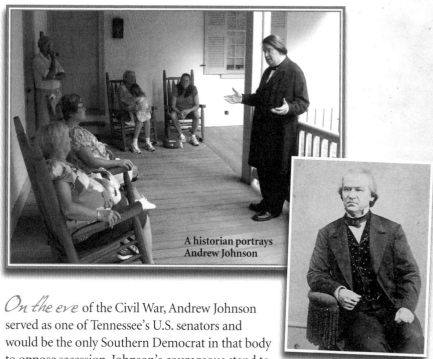

A historian portrays
Andrew Johnson

On the eve of the Civil War, Andrew Johnson served as one of Tennessee's U.S. senators and would be the only Southern Democrat in that body to oppose secession. Johnson's courageous stand to keep Tennessee in the Union made him a popular figure in the North during the war. His loyalty to the Union cause led to his appointment by Abraham Lincoln as Tennessee's military governor in 1862. Johnson's work as a War Democrat to restore Tennessee to the Union resulted in his nomination as Lincoln's vice-president in 1864.

Andrew Johnson NHS presents the 17th president to visitors as a man of great complexity and personal integrity. His impeachment, trial, and acquittal took place during the turmoil of Reconstruction. Johnson's defense of the Constitution helped preserve the balance of power between the branches of the Federal government. His rise from tailor to president is a shining example of the American ideal and the success open to the common man. The site is made up of two of his homes, a visitor center, and a national cemetery. These areas stitch together a story of a nation in transition: Civil War, emancipation, and westward expansion.

In February 1862, a joint Union navy and army expedition moved against the western Confederate defense line in Tennessee and netted three forts, control of two major rivers, and 13,000 Confederate prisoners.

Gen. Ulysses S. Grant was given permission to attack Confederate Forts Henry and Heiman with naval forces under Flag Officer Andrew H. Foote, commander of the newly constructed ironclad gunboats. By February 6, Grant's forces were in place, and he ordered the attack. As Confederate Gen. Lloyd Tilghman had about 3,500 men against Grant's 15,000 and Foote's gunboats, and Fort Henry was partially flooded, he ordered both forts abandoned. Leaving enough men to man the heavy guns, the others escaped to Fort Donelson. The battle lasted about an hour, and Fort Henry surrendered to the navy before the Union army arrived. The Tennessee River was open, Union vessels steamed to Alabama, and Grant began making plans to take Fort Donelson.

By February 11, Grant's army began marching to Fort Donelson. On February 12 and 13, they

Dover Hotel

surrounded and probed the Confederate works to prevent any escapes. By afternoon on February 14, everybody was in place—about 17,000 Confederate forces and Grant's army of about 27,000. The gunboats were ordered forward. Fort Donelson, built on much higher ground than Fort Henry, was harder for the gunboats to attack. In less than two hours, the gunboats were so damaged they had to retreat. Although the fort was still surrounded, Confederate Generals Floyd, Pillow, and Buckner decided the best option was to break through Grant's lines and escape.

The attack at daybreak on February 14 caught Union forces by surprise, forcing them back and opening escape routes. But the generals failed to take advantage of this, returning to their trenches. Grant took this opportunity to reoccupy much of the lost ground and attack, ultimately demanding unconditional surrender and earning the nickname "Unconditional Surrender" Grant. At day's end, the Confederates were back inside with a portion of their works captured by Union forces. General Buckner made the surrender, and 13,000 Confederate prisoners began their trip to Northern prisons. The Cumberland River was open to invasion, Nashville was occupied by the North, the gate to the Confederate heartland was open and the Union army poured in.

Shiloh National Military Park

1055 Pittsburg Landing Road • Shiloh, TN 38376 • 731-689-5696

This culturally diverse park encompasses the well preserved Shiloh Battlefield in southwest Tennessee, and numerous sites associated with the Siege and Battle of Corinth in northeast Mississippi, including Davis Bridge battlefield near Pocahontas, Tennessee. Visitors enjoy ample opportunities to explore the provocative military history preserved and commemorated on two of the horrendous killing fields of the American Civil War (momentous Shiloh, fought April 6-7, and Corinth, October 3-4, 1862), and delve into the complex issues, causes, and consequences of the war as the defining crossroads in the American experience. The eight-month contest in 1862 waged for the control of Corinth, the most important railroad transportation hub in the Western Confederacy,

Minnesota Monument

Men of the 7th Illinois Infantry who fought at Corinth

Morning muster during anniversary program

proved decisive. The bloody battles of Shiloh and Corinth claimed a combined 36,000 casualties, significantly influencing military events in the West, where Federal forces successfully maneuvered to sever the Confederacy by seizing control of the Mississippi River.

Visitor facilities at the 4,200-acre Shiloh Battlefield include the park visitor center and a bookstore located at Pittsburg Landing. The center offers an orientation film and artifact exhibits, and serves as the primary location for information on the battlefield, which also preserves the burials of nearly 6,000 U.S. and Confederate soldiers, over 200 cannon, and 900 monuments and markers.

The Corinth Battlefield Unit preserves over 800 acres of historic sites, battlefields, and field fortifications associated with the siege, battle, and military occupation of this Southern town, including the site of the Corinth contraband camp which commemorates the history of African Americans progressing from slave to freeman to soldier. Visits begin at the Corinth Civil War Interpretive Center, where interactive audio-visual presentations and exhibits explore the key role Corinth played during the war.

STONES RIVER NATIONAL BATTLEFIELD

3501 Old Nashville Highway • Murfreesboro, TN 37129 • 615-893-9501

Near the end of 1862, President Lincoln was desperate for a military victory to bolster the will of the Northern people and to support the Emancipation Proclamation as it went into effect on January 1, 1863. By the end of 1862, Lincoln's hopes rested with Gen. William S. Rosecrans and the 43,000-man Army of the Cumberland. Gen. Braxton Bragg and his 38,000-man Army of Tennessee waited in camp ready to defend middle Tennessee. On December 30, 1862, the armies faced each other in the fields and forests west of Murfreesboro, and both commanders planned for the coming battle.

At first light the last day of 1862, a gray tide swept over the Federals, shattering the Union right flank. The Federals slowed down the Confederate

advance near their center as the morning progressed. The bloody fighting in the rocks and trees led soldiers to call this place the "Slaughter Pen." As morning passed, Rosecrans formed a new defensive line anchored

Reenactor drills new recruits

on the Round Forest where Col. William B. Hazen's brigade repulsed four Confederate attacks. The fire of Union artillery along the Nashville Pike devastated each Confederate thrust through the afternoon. The day ended with the Army of the Cumberland clinging to its lifeline and the exhausted Confederates confident they would soon claim victory.

After a quiet New Year's Day, Bragg ordered Gen. John C. Breckinridge to attack Union forces near Stones River on January 2, 1863. At 4 p.m., Breckinridge's 3,500 men charged the Union lines and took the high ground. Union cannon pummeled the Confederates as they pressed towards the river. Breckinridge's men wavered then broke, leaving 1,800 dead and wounded.

The Battle of Stones River was over. Nearly 24,000 men were dead, wounded, or captured. In the months following, the Federals built Fortress Rosecrans and turned Murfreesboro into a forward supply base to support their campaigns through Chattanooga and Atlanta. Lincoln got the success he needed, calling it "a hard-earned victory, which had there been a defeat instead, the country scarcely could have lived over."

Gen. William S. Rosecrans

Gen. Braxton Bragg

Use this page for cancellations or field notes.

Fort Davis National Historic Site

101 Lt. Henry Flipper Drive • P.O. Box 1379 • Fort Davis, TX 79734 • 432-426-3225

Artillery demonstration

Texas seceded from the Union on March 4, 1861, and joined the Confederacy on March 23. State commissioners demanded the surrender of Federal military property and the withdrawal of Federal troops. Gen. David Twiggs met the demand on February 18. Orders promptly went out for the evacuation of the frontier forts. On April 13, Fort Davis was abandoned. The 2nd Texas Mounted Rifles under Lt. Col. John R. Baylor passed Fort Davis in June 1861. Company D of the regiment, officered by Lts. Reuben E. Mays and W. P. White, held Fort Davis. In August, Apaches raided Fort Davis. With 14 men, Lieutenant Mays followed the trail. On August 12, the Confederate detachment rode into the ambush. All the soldiers were killed. Only the Mexican guide escaped to tell the story.

Gen. Henry Sibley's brigade passed through Fort Davis in November 1861. It won victory at Valverde and seized Albuquerque and Santa Fe only to be turned back in March at the Battle of Glorieta Pass. Many of the wounded were sent to Fort Davis, which became a medical receiving station. General Sibley withdrew from New Mexico and West Texas. His regiments passed Fort Davis early in August, taking the small garrison with them. On August 27, 1862, a detachment of Federal cavalry rode cautiously into Fort Davis. The U.S. flag flew again over Fort Davis for one day, and then the Federals marched back to Fort Bliss. Fort Davis lay deserted for the next five years.

GOLDEN SPIKE NATIONAL HISTORIC SITE

P.O. Box 897 • Brigham City, UT 84302 • 435-471-2209

Promontory Summit,
May 10, 1869

The idea of a transcontinental railroad was thought of long before the Civil War. However, no one could decide on a proper route as Southerners wanted a southern route and, of course, Northerners wanted a northern route. Abraham Lincoln also wanted a route because it would allow troops to be sent from the East Coast to the West Coast in about a week instead of four to six months.

In 1862, with the Civil War in progress, the idea of a southern route became less desirable and the Pacific Railroad Act was passed by Congress. This act formed the Union Pacific Railroad and allowed its counterpart, the Central Pacific, which already had organized in California, to begin construction of the transcontinental railroad. However, construction was delayed until after the war as supplies and labor were hard to come by. Construction began in earnest after the war with many Civil War veterans getting jobs working for the railroad companies. This massive effort led to the completion of the country's first transcontinental railroad and the "driving" of the golden spike at Promontory Summit, Utah Territory, on May 10, 1869. The completion of the railroad led to the unification and expansion of America as the dreams of Manifest Destiny were realized.

Civil War veterans, Woodstock, 1907

Marsh-Billings-Rockefeller NHP offers one of the first National Park Service programs interpreting the Civil War home front. This program includes a guided walking tour through Woodstock, Vermont's historic streets, including sites associated with the Underground Railroad, abolition meetings, the town's free African American community, and its service with the 54th Massachusetts Regiment. Park staff worked side by side with student interns combing home front records, from the basement of the Woodstock Historical Society to the pension files of the National Archives. What they developed is a story of suffering, perseverance, and higher moral purpose. It is story of a world turned upside down that profoundly transformed Vermont and a story of why public memory of the war and its causes and consequences—always contested—still matters today.

On the afternoon of April 8, 1865, supply trains awaited General Lee's army at Appomattox Station. Federal Gen. George Custer pushed his division forward and captured the trains. Then Custer's men made several mounted charges through wooded terrain into a clearing where Confederate Gen. Reuben Walker deployed 25-30 cannon in a semi-circle. The first two charges were repulsed largely with the use of canister, but a final charge netted 25 cannon, 200 wagons, and some 1,000 prisoners. The success of the Federal troops that evening was vital. The Federals held the high ground west of Appomattox Court House, squarely across Lee's line of march.

With Lee's line of retreat blocked, his only options on April 9, 1865, were to attack or surrender. After holding a Council of War, Lee elected to attack, believing it only to be Federal cavalry blocking the way. However, during the night, parts of three Federal corps made a forced march and were close at hand to support the Federal cavalry in the morning.

That night, a Federal cavalry brigade occupied the ridge west of Appomattox Court House. On the morning of April 9, Gen. John B. Gordon's Confederate infantry and Gen. Fitzhugh Lee's cavalry advanced from the village and succeeded in driving the Federal cavalry from the ridge, but the success was

The surrender scene depicted by Louis Guillaume

McLean House

fleeting as the Federal
Army of the James arrived
on the field to the west,
and the Federal 5th Corps
advanced from the south.
To Lee's rear was the
Federal Army of the Potomac. He was effectively surrounded, "check-mated."

The horrific all-out final battle that many feared did not come as the
advantage of position gained by the action on April 8 and movements on
April 9 gave Grant's forces control of the strategic ground necessary to force Lee's
surrender. Yet casualties of these two battles have been estimated at 500 killed
and wounded, and over 1,000 men captured in the two days of fighting. Within
hours, Lee and Grant met at the home of Wilmer McLean in the village of
Appomattox Court House. It was a meeting that
not only resulted in the surrender of the Army
of Northern Virginia, but set the future course
of the country, and the dawn of peace.

The park interprets the events of
April 1865 through displays, wayside exhibits,
ranger and living history talks, and several
documentary programs.

Use this page for cancellations or field notes.

c/o George Washington Memorial Parkway • Arlington, VA 22101 • 703-235-1530

Arlington House, The Robert E. Lee Memorial, was the home of Robert E. Lee and his family between 1831 and 1861. Robert E. Lee's father-in-law, George Washington Parke Custis, built the house in sections between 1802 and 1818 as a memorial to his step-grandfather, George Washington. Lee married Custis's daughter, Mary, in 1831, and they would go on to raise seven children of their own. On April 20, 1861, Lee faced a difficult decision. He was offered command of Union troops in Washington, D.C., to defend the capital; however, Virginia had already seceded from the Union. Lee was a 32-year veteran in the U.S. Army, but was first and foremost loyal to his home state of Virginia. He could not raise his sword against his home and family. Lee wrote his letter of resignation in his bedchamber. He left Arlington House two days later, never to return.

Union troops crossed the Potomac in May 1861, and occupied the estate, using the house as army headquarters. By the spring of 1864, the city of Washington was struggling to bury the mounting Civil War dead. Two hundred acres of the Arlington estate were set aside as a military cemetery for the Union dead. In 1925, Congress designated Arlington House as a memorial to Lee, very much for his work to rebuild the nation after the war.

12130 Booker T. Washington Highway • Hardy, VA 24101 • 540-721-2094

Tobacco farmer James Burroughs, his wife, Elizabeth, and their children moved to Franklin County, Virginia, with their slaves, including Jane, who would become Booker T. Washington's mother on April 5, 1856. Jane was the cook, and in 1861, when Burroughs died, there were 10 slaves on the 207-acre plantation. During the Civil War, five of Burroughs' sons joined the Confederate army. Mrs. Burroughs, her daughters, and her slaves were left to work the farm. Booker and his family lived in the kitchen cabin adjacent to the Big House.

In 1865, the war ended. Booker wrote, "The most distinct thing that I now recall in connection with the scene was that some man…made a speech and then read a rather long paper—the Emancipation Proclamation, I think. After the reading we were told that we were all free, and could go when and where we pleased. The wild rejoicing…lasted but for a brief period, for I noticed that by the time they returned to their cabins there was a change in their feelings. The great responsibility of being free, of having charge of themselves, of having to think and plan for themselves and their children, seemed to take possession of them."

Booker T. Washington National Monument celebrates Booker T. Washington's "first breath of freedom" with its annual *Juneteenth* event on the third Saturday in June.

7718 1/2 Main Street • P.O. Box 700 • Middletown, VA 22645 • 540-868-9176

Following his victories in September and October 1864, Maj. Gen. Philip Sheridan and his Army of the Shenandoah conducted a systematic destruction of a 75-mile swath of the Shenandoah Valley. "The Burning" essentially laid waste to the "Breadbasket of the Confederacy." Confident the campaign was over, Sheridan camped his army north of Cedar Creek before traveling to Washington, D.C. The poorly equipped Confederate Army of the Valley, led by Lt. Gen. Jubal Early, seemed to pose little threat. Desperate to achieve a victory, Early and his commanders devised a daring plan to attack Sheridan. After an all-night march, the Confederates rolled out of a dense fog in the pre-dawn hours of October 19. The Confederate onslaught overran the Federals and drove past the Belle Grove Plantation. By 10:30 a.m., the stunned Union army was in full retreat.

Sheridan's Ride

Belle Grove Mansion

Sheridan, riding from Winchester that morning, was completely unaware of the disaster that had befallen his army. Upon hearing the growing sounds of battle, he quickened his pace and rode hard to the field. "Sheridan's Ride" forever cemented his status in American history. Rallying his defeated forces, he ordered a counterattack at 4:00 p.m. that swept the Confederates from the field. Total casualties numbered approximately 5,700 Federals and 2,900 Confederates. Early's army was shattered, and with it further Confederate resistance in the Valley ended. Occurring just three weeks before the presidential election, the Battle of Cedar Creek gave sagging Northern morale a much-needed boost and helped carry Abraham Lincoln to a landslide victory at the polls.

FREDERICKSBURG AND SPOTSYLVANIA NATIONAL MILITARY PARK

120 Chatham Lane • Fredericksburg, VA 22405 • 540-373-6122

No place in America saw such concentrated combat as Fredericksburg, Virginia, and its surrounding counties. Between December 1862 and May 1864, the Union and Confederate armies fought four major battles in the area, resulting in more than 100,000 casualties.

Fredericksburg itself is the most famous of the four battles. In December 1862, Union General Ambrose E. Burnside brought the 115,000-man Army of the Potomac to the banks of the Rappahannock River in an effort to defeat Robert E. Lee's 75,000-man Army of Northern Virginia and capture Richmond. Burnside's ill-advised assaults against Lee's strong position behind the town, however, resulted in one of the most lopsided Confederate victories of the war.

General Joseph Hooker replaced Burnside as the Army of the Potomac's commander. In April 1863, Hooker crossed the Rappahannock River again, engaging Lee at a rural crossroads known as Chancellorsville. Although heavily outnumbered, Lee outfought and outmaneuvered his opponent, winning the greatest victory of his career. The triumph came at great cost, however, for his stellar subordinate, General "Stonewall" Jackson, was mortally wounded in the battle, dying eight days later at Guinea Station.

Battle of Fredericksburg, by John Richards, ca. 1862

Bed where Stonewall Jackson died

One year after Hooker's defeat at Chancellorsville, the two armies collided again, this time a few miles west of Chancellorsville in the tangled woodlands of the Wilderness. When the muzzle flashes of rifles set the woods on fire, dozens, if not hundreds, of wounded men perished in the flames. Still the fighting raged.

Unable to defeat the Confederates in the Wilderness, Union commander General Ulysses S. Grant slid south and attacked Lee again, this time at Spotsylvania Court House. Two weeks of combat reached its grisly apogee on May 12, 1864, at the "Bloody Angle." In a day of fighting unparalleled in American history, Union and Confederate soldiers struggled for 22 hours in a pouring rain, their corpses piling up two, three, even four deep in front of the Confederate defenses. Despite the unprecedented carnage, neither side could claim victory.

Today, at approximately 8,000 acres, Fredericksburg and Spotsylvania County Battlefields National Military Park is one of the world's largest battlefield parks. Its two visitor centers, four historic buildings, and miles of tour roads and walking trails provide abundant opportunity for visitors to explore the grounds that decided the fate of a nation.

Use this page for cancellations or field notes.

Use this page for cancellations or field notes.

Manassas NBP preserves over 5,000 acres of two significant battlefields of the Civil War. It was at Manassas that Confederate Brig. Gen. Thomas J. Jackson acquired his nickname "Stonewall." On July 21, 1861, the First Battle of Manassas, or Bull Run, erupted on the plains of Manassas along the banks of Bull Run in what the contending Union and Confederate armies naively believed would be the only battle of the war. After 10 hours of stubborn, savage combat, some 900 soldiers were killed, the Union army was in rout, stampeding back to Washington, and the exhausted Confederates held the bloody field. The romantic

Henry Hill Monument

illusions of battle as a glorious spectacle and entertainment were drowned in the bloody reality of 5,000 casualties. Both Union and Confederate armies suffered the death of innocence in the first major battle of the war, as the realization dawned that the struggle would be a protracted slaughter.

Thirteen months later, from August 28-30, 1862, veteran armies again clashed in the same pastures and woodlots near the

Henry Hill

Stone House, ca. late 1860s

creek of Bull Run. The enthusiasm of the raw recruits of the previous summer had been extinguished in the grim sacrifice and suffering of a year of fratricidal war. A firm perseverance had supplanted the naïve attitudes of a year ago in the seasoned soldiers of the Union and Confederate armies. For two and a half days, carnage of a savagery seldom before experienced raged in the battle, which killed 3,300. Some 24,000 casualties were suffered in the combat along the cuts and fills of an unfinished railroad and on the naked ridges and hills of the battlefield. The Union army was again defeated, but rather than in humiliated rout, it withdrew in disciplined retreat to Washington. The Confederate victory was the prelude to the first invasion of the North, repulsed at the bloodbath of Antietam on September 17, 1862, in the war's bloodiest day.

1539 Hickory Hill Road • Petersburg, VA 23803 • 804-732-3531

Dead Confederate soldier, April 1865

Taylor House remains

The Union army waged a 10-month campaign from 1864 to 1865 to seize Petersburg.

Opening Attacks – June 15-18, 1864: Grant pulled his army out of Cold Harbor and crossed the James River heading towards Petersburg. For several days Lee did not believe Grant's main target was Petersburg and so kept most of his army around Richmond. Between June 15-18, 1864, Grant threw his forces against Petersburg and it may have fallen if it were not for the Federal commanders failing to press their advantage and the defense put up by the few Confederates holding the lines. Lee finally arrived on June 18, and after four days of combat with no success, Grant began siege operations.

Battle of the Crater – July 30, 1864: Union troops exploded a mine under Elliott's Salient of the Confederate line. Union troops belonging to General Burnside's IX Corps charged forward hoping to break into Petersburg, but the attack failed miserably.

Battle of Weldon Railroad – August 18-21, 1864: Union troops attacked and took control of one of Petersburg's most important railroads.

Battle of Fort Stedman – March 25, 1864: By mid-March it was apparent to Lee that Grant's superior force would either get around the Confederate right flank or pierce the line somewhere along its 37-mile length. The Southern commanders hoped to break the Union stranglehold on Petersburg by a surprise attack on Grant. This resulted in the Confederate loss at Fort Stedman and would be Lee's last grand offensive of the war.

The Forlorn Hope
by Don Troiani

The Battle of Five Forks – April 1, 1865: With victory near, Grant unleashed General Phillip Sheridan at Five Forks on April 1, 1865. His objective was the South Side Railroad, the last rail line into Petersburg. Sheridan, with the V Corps, smashed the Confederate forces under General George Pickett and opened access to the tracks beyond. On April 2, Grant ordered an all-out assault, and Lee's right flank crumbled. A Homeric defense at Confederate Fort Gregg saved Lee from possible street fighting in Petersburg. On the night of April 2, Lee evacuated Petersburg. The final surrender at Appomattox Court House was but a week away.

A visitor contact station is located just to the south of Five Forks, along Courthouse Road and features artifacts, displays, and a video.

Use this page for cancellations or field notes.

Use this page for cancellations or field notes.

Drewry's Bluff cannon crew demonstration

Tredegar Ironworks

"On to Richmond!" The cry went up throughout the Northern states in the spring of 1861, urging Federal troops onto the newly named capital of the Confederate States of America to quell an infant rebellion by 11 Southern states that had seceded from the United States after decades of sectional strife. Ultimately, four long years would pass, and more than 620,000 troops on both sides would perish before Federal troops entered Richmond, effectively bringing an end to the Civil War. Today, at Richmond National Battlefield Park, you will find many opportunities to visit the sites where these defining events of our nation occurred and learn the stories of the soldiers and civilians who struggled to survive in and around the wartime capital.

The park was established in 1936 to preserve important battlefields of the campaigns to capture Richmond. Eleven of the park's 13 units preserve four significant Civil War campaigns, including the May 15, 1862 naval engagement at Drewry's Bluff; the 1862 Seven Days' Battles (at Beaver Dam Creek, Gaines'

Mill, Glendale and Malvern Hill battlefields); the 1864 Overland Campaign at Totopotomoy Creek and Cold Harbor; and actions during the Richmond-Petersburg Campaign, from September 29, 1864 to April 2, 1865, encompassing Fort Harrison and Parker's Battery.

Begin your visit at the Tredegar Visitor Center, located in one of the original buildings of the Confederacy's most famous ironworks. Here, exhibits and audio-visual programs tell the story of the battles and provide information and maps to tour the battlefields and other Civil War sites around the city. Also at Tredegar is the American Civil War Center, operated by a National Park Service partner, whose museum is the first in the nation to interpret the Civil War from the Union, Confederate, and African American perspectives.

Gaines' Mill battlefield

Old Cold Harbor tavern

In addition to Tredegar, the park includes four additional visitor centers, located at Cold Harbor, Glendale/Malvern Hill, Fort Harrison, and Chimborazo. The Chimborazo Visitor Center also houses a medical museum where the Confederate medical story is presented on the site of Chimborazo Hospital, the Confederacy's largest such operation. Throughout the year, national park rangers present a variety of talks, tours, living history demonstrations, and special events that commemorate the park's rich heritage.

Confederate battery

Yorktown National Cemetery

The allied victory of the Siege of Yorktown in 1781 effectively ended the American Revolutionary War. During the 1862 Peninsula Campaign of the Civil War, Yorktown was again the site of major siege operations. Yorktown is located along the York River on a peninsula that leads to Richmond, then the Confederate capital. In May 1861, Confederate forces under Gen. John B. Magruder began fortifying the peninsula and Yorktown, where his troops reinforced some of the 1781 earthworks. The following April, the Army of the Potomac under Gen. George B. McClellan, deployed from Federally controlled Fort Monroe, located at the tip of the peninsula. Encountering the Confederate defenses, McClellan prepared to besiege Yorktown, building 15 siege batteries and extensive earthworks. By May 3, 1862, over 100 siege cannon were aimed at Yorktown. That same night, the Confederates, anticipating an imminent massive bombardment, evacuated their lines. The next morning, Union troops entered the town. Citing Yorktown's strategic position for possible future campaigns and the need to possess the 1781 battlefield to "avoid the moral effect of abandoning a place … familiar to the whole Country through its historic associations," Union troops garrisoned Yorktown for the rest of the war.

The National Park Service commemorates Yorktown's Civil War history with special programs and tactical demonstrations every Memorial Day weekend.

Harpers Ferry National Historical Park

West Virginia

171 Shoreline Drive • P.O. Box 65 • Harpers Ferry, WV 25425 • 304-535-6029

Firing demonstration

John Brown launched his war against slavery when he attacked the U.S. armory and arsenal at Harpers Ferry in October 1859. The fiery abolitionist failed when he was captured by U.S. Marines led by Robert E. Lee. Brown soon was executed, but he helped spur the Civil War that entrapped Harpers Ferry on the border between North and South.

Harpers Ferry changed hands eight times during the Civil War. Situated at the gateway into the Shenandoah Valley, both sides coveted Harpers Ferry's strategic location. The Federals used the town for a supply base, launching repeated invasions from here into the heart of Virginia. The Confederates targeted this area as a dagger into the United States, spearheading armies into Northern territory.

The most famous battle occurred in mid-September, 1862, during the Confederacy's first invasion of the North. Confederate General Stonewall Jackson seized the mountains and surrounded the outnumbered Union garrison during a three-day siege. Jackson forced the surrender of nearly 12,700 Federal soldiers—the largest capitulation of U.S. troops during the Civil War. Jackson's Harpers Ferry victory enabled Robert E. Lee to make a stand along Antietam Creek a few days later.

Ft. Pulaski contraband camp

The Underground Railroad—the resistance to enslavement through escape and flight, through the end of the Civil War—refers to the efforts of enslaved African Americans to gain their freedom by escaping bondage. Wherever slavery existed, there were efforts to escape, at first to communities in rugged terrain away from settled areas, and later across state and international borders. While most began and completed their journeys unassisted, each subsequent decade in which slavery was legal in the United States saw an increase in active efforts to assist escape. The decision to assist a freedom seeker may have been spontaneous. However, in some places, particularly after the Fugitive Slave Act of 1850, the Underground Railroad was deliberate and organized.

The National Underground Railroad Network to Freedom commemorates the stories of the men and women who risked everything for freedom, and those who helped them. The Network to Freedom, through shared leadership with local, state, and federal entities, as well as interested individuals and organizations, promotes programs and partnerships to commemorate and educate the public about the historical significance of the UGRR.

The Underground Railroad extended through the Civil War as thousands of enslaved African Americans used the opportunity of approaching Union forces to escape and seek protection in contraband camps. Many of the men subsequently enlisted in the U.S. Colored Troops and served as soldiers or sailors during the war. A number of Network to Freedom sites recognize this history.

*For more information, visit **www.nps.gov/ugrr***

Use this page for cancellations or field notes.

Use this page for cancellations or field notes.